MARY BERRY
EVERYDAY

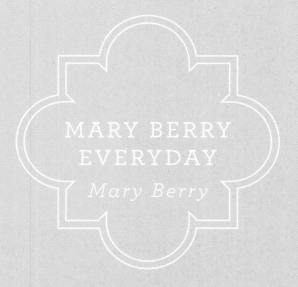

MARY BERRY
EVERYDAY

Mary Berry

BBC
BOOKS

1 3 5 7 9 10 8 6 4 2

BBC Books, an imprint of Ebury Publishing
20 Vauxhall Bridge Road,
London SW1V 2SA

BBC Books is part of the Penguin Random House group of companies whose addresses can be found at global

penguinrandomhouse.com

Photography by Georgia Glynn Smith

This book is published to accompany the television series entitled Mary Berry Everyday first broadcast
on BBC Two in 2016. Mary Berry Everyday is a Sidney Street TV production.

BBC Commissioning Executive: Tom Edwards
Series Director: David Crerar
Series Producer: Emma Boswell
Executive producer: Karen Ross
Production Manager: Emily Shield
Production Co-ordinator: Kat Furner

First published by BBC Books in 2017

www.eburypublishing.co.uk

A CIP catalogue record for this book is available from the British Library

ISBN 9781785941689

Editorial Director: Lizzy Gray
Project Editor: Charlotte Macdonald
Food Stylists: Lisa Harrison, Isla Murray
Prop Stylist: Jo Harris
Design: Lucy Stephens
Testing: Jan Fullwood, Anne Harnan
Copyeditor: Kate Parker
Production: Helen Everson

Colour origination by Altaimage, London

Printed and bound in Italy by L.E.G.O. S.p.A

Penguin Random House is committed to a sustainable future for our business, our readers and our planet.
This book is made from Forest Stewardship Council® certified paper.

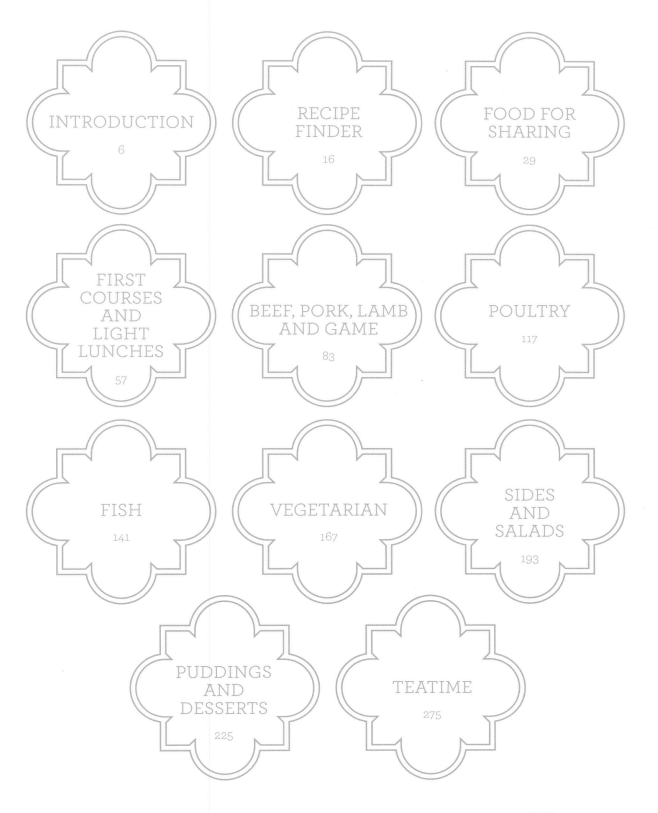

INTRODUCTION

Cooking every day for yourself and the family means preparing dishes that are both straightforward and enjoyable to make. The inspiration behind this new collection of recipes that I've put together is just that: dishes made using everyday ingredients, for easy preparation and cooking, but often with a simple twist to give interest and variety.

Organising meals and preparing food can be quite a balancing act: with all the demands of a busy life, you need to be able to cook without thinking to some extent, yet you don't want to get stuck in a rut, producing the same dishes day in day out. You need fresh ideas but nothing so unusual that it means spending a great deal of time and effort in the kitchen. This new collection of recipes is all about making everyday dishes that little bit different but with the minimum of fuss. Food does not have to be complicated to taste and look great, so I've tried to ensure that each ingredient list is as short as possible and that it uses familiar ingredients rather than anything too obscure or tricky to source. Just using familiar ingredients in a different way can make a weekday meal a bit more special or give added oomph to a dish for a special occasion and still be healthy.

So many more ingredients are available these days, compared with when I first started cooking, that it is not difficult making adaptations to your cooking. New ingredients soon cease to be faddish and become familiar. It wasn't so long ago that bulgar wheat was an unusual ingredient, for instance, but now that's regarded as a staple, and quinoa is fast becoming one too. You'll see that I've used a mixture of both grains in two delicious, super-healthy salads – the Herbed Quinoa and Bulgar Wheat Salad with Lemon and Pomegranate on page 217 and the Warm Bulgar Wheat and Quinoa Broccoli Salad on page 22. British food today reflects influences from a wide range of different cultures, making it easy to inject variety into your cooking, from Mexican-inspired chilli dishes, including the chicken samosas on page 45, to touches of Asian cuisine, as you'll see in dishes like my Fragrant Light Prawn Curry on page 155 or the Crispy-skinned Duck Breasts with Pak Choi and Pineapple Sauce on page 138.

Asian-inspired recipes can be the best ones to turn to when time is short. Stir-fry dishes are tailor-made for the busy cook: as well as being very healthy for you, with all those lightly cooked vegetables, they are full of lovely fresh flavour and varied texture. I've included a few of them in this collection, such as the Chicken Stir-fry with Teriyaki Sauce on page 126 or my Five Spice Salmon Stir-fry on page 154. Moving from the Orient to the Mediterranean, pasta is super-quick too, of course – wonderfully comforting as well as richly flavoursome. It makes an excellent

vegetarian option – see my Fresh and Sun-dried Tomato Pasta with Mozzarella and Basil on page 171, for instance, or the creamy Orzo with Broad Beans, Peas, Lemon and Thyme on page 185 for a tasty alternative to risotto.

Speedy dishes are all-important, but everyday cooking is also about giving pleasure to others, your family and friends, and I've included some old favourites here, from cottage pie and beef stew to Chicken Dijon and Lamb Fricassee with Pearl Barley (see pages 115, 87, 129 and 112). But even well-loved dishes can be jazzed up a little bit to keep them interesting. For a change, I've made the cottage pie with venison rather than beef mince, for its lean meat with deeper flavour and colour. My Beef and Ale Stew with Horseradish Dumplings is hearty and warming, perfect for feeding a crowd, but the dumplings, cut in cross-section, form lovely spirals from the horseradish sauce – sure to delight your guests. Meanwhile, the Smoked Haddock and Cauliflower Gratin on page 156 is effectively two dishes in one: fish pie and cauliflower cheese. A combination of two comforting classics, it is bound to go down well.

And for finishing off a meal, what gives greater pleasure than a delicious pud? Puddings and desserts may not be something you produce every day, but they can provide a much-needed touch of indulgence, from a simple rice pudding or crumble (see pages 229 and 233) to a show-stopping dessert like Paris–Brest, a decadent 'wheel' of cream-filled, ganache-covered choux pastry (see page 255), or the White Chocolate and Raspberry Cheesecake (see page 247) with its lovely contrasts in colour and texture.

When it comes to saving time, why not let your oven do the work for you? A long cooking time in a recipe shouldn't put you off making it as it means that, once you've popped the dish in the oven, you can then forget about it for a while and spend your time doing other things. In the meantime, the oven works its magic to blend flavours together and wonderfully improve them. My Chilli con Carne on page 89 may not seem so different, but the long, slow cooking makes it meltingly tasty; even better if you prepare it a day ahead. For a vegetarian option, there's the Squash and Black Bean Chilli on page 179, using black beans instead of the more standard kidney beans, or the gorgeous Melanzane Pasta on page 180, with its delicious layers of lasagne, béchamel sauce and aubergine – one of my favourite dishes for preparing ahead, and adding pasta to the aubergine classic makes it a great family bake.

Entertaining guests is more about cooking once in a while than every day, but with a bit of forward planning, it can be worked into your daily routine without too much hassle. Many of the starters and sharing dishes included in this book can be knocked up in minutes yet look impressive too – such as the vibrant Beetroot

Houmous on page 52 or the Thai Crab Poppadom Canapés on page 34. Others can be prepared well in advance, such as the spectacular Two-sided Herbed Smoked Salmon and Horseradish Pâté on page 72. I've included a number of suitable main dishes that can be prepared in an hour or less, and there are some ultra-quick puddings too, such as the Mojito Cheesecakes or Scots Whisky Cream on pages 259 and 270.

To help you get the best out of each recipe and build up a repertoire of helpful tricks and techniques, I've included a wealth of tips, at least one to accompany each recipe. For this new collection, I've also provided a recipe finder (see pages 16–18) to help you locate the dishes that are best suited to your needs according to the occasion and the time you have available, along with some sample menu plans (see pages 20–21). In addition, each recipe includes preparation or cooking times, so you can see at a glance how best to fit it into your day. In the section that follows this introduction, I've also laid out a few general tips on planning your meals – as important, in my view, as the ingredients you select – and some guidelines about choosing ingredients to ensure the best results from your cooking.

Having everything to hand is so helpful, too. This is where your store cupboard and freezer come into their own, as you'll see in the sections on pages 22–23 and 24–27. Do take a quick look through these pages to see what might be useful to stock up on before you embark on the recipes themselves. Having a full range of spices makes cooking any kind of curry or spicy dish so much easier, for instance. And did you know that, with a little preparation, you can freeze most fresh fruit and vegetables, including herbs? Fresh herbs can be frozen in small portions and defrosted quickly. Like spices, they can make all the difference to a recipe, whether in delicious sauces or dressings or just added as a garnish at the end. Fish also freezes well and if you keep a packet of panko breadcrumbs in your store cupboard, or a bag of whizzed-up breadcrumbs in your freezer, you are well on the way to making the Very Posh Fishcakes (see page 145), crisp on the outside and with a gorgeous tangy sauce within, or the homemade Fish and Chips with Tartare Sauce (see page 147) – much better than any takeaway!

I do hope you enjoy the recipes I've brought together here as much as I've enjoyed developing them. And I hope, by trying them, that you will feel encouraged to liven up your own cooking and experiment with different techniques, giving you the confidence you need to step out of your comfort zone, expand your repertoire and create dishes that will become your own family favourites, making everyday meals into something extra special.

Mary Berry

EVERYDAY COOKING

For me, the first and crucial step in making everyday cooking easier is to put more time and effort into forward planning and preparation. You'll find that it pays dividends by making you into a better and more confident cook too. I'm a firm believer in preparing ahead: the more organised and efficient you can be as a cook, the more likely it is that the finished dish will look and taste delicious. If you have a clear idea of the finished dish before you start cooking, ensure you have the correct ingredients to hand and set aside enough time to cook, you are almost guaranteed to create something special.

The second step to better cooking is all about flavour and presentation. Learn to trust your judgement – this does take time and practice but it can only improve with experience and by exploring new dishes. Flavour, texture, colour and seasoning are the four most important factors in any dish. Always taste your dishes before serving and adjust the seasoning accordingly.

STEP 1: HOW TO BE AN ORGANISED COOK

Planning ahead makes life so much easier, giving you time to cook without feeling rushed. Here are a few time-saving tips to help you become better prepared and more relaxed in the kitchen.

Meal planning: *It is a good idea to plan the week's meals ahead, if you can. This means that you need spend less time shopping day to day, giving yourself more time to cook. It also gives you more time for yourself. With this in mind, I've devised a few menu plans, based on recipes in this book, that you might like to try – see pages 20–21.*

Recipe checklist: *If you are following a new recipe, read it carefully before shopping to ensure that you have all the ingredients and equipment you need before you begin cooking.*

Store cupboard: *Keep a well-stocked store cupboard and top up essentials on a monthly basis in order to keep shopping trips to a minimum. If it is well stocked, you should only need to shop for fresh ingredients during the week. See pages 22–23 for a list of items that I keep in my own store cupboard and 'Simple Ways to Boost Flavour' below for a little more detail about some of them.*

Make the most of your freezer: *Used cleverly, the freezer can save you time, money and reduce the stress of cooking day to day. It offers multi-purpose storage, enabling you to keep handy ingredients for weekday meals, such as stock, extra pints of milk or homemade breadcrumbs, and prepare dishes ahead if you're planning a celebration. For general tips on what to freeze and how to organise your freezer, see pages 24–27.*

Batch cooking: *If you're making a casserole, soup or stew, it's always worth making extra so that you can freeze portions to enjoy at a later date.*

STEP 2: HOW TO MAKE THINGS
TASE AND LOOK BETTER

SELECTING INGREDIENTS

Buy the best ingredients you can afford: *The quality of the ingredients you use is key to the success of your finished dish. If you begin with great-tasting, fresh ingredients, the resulting dish is much more likely to taste good too. Buy the freshest fruit and veg you can find locally, or you may be lucky enough to grow your own. Choose British meat and sustainably sourced fish.*

Eat seasonally: *Fruit and vegetables are at their very best when in season, and they have so much more flavour, crunch and vibrancy, which allows you to keep recipes simple and let the taste of the ingredients shine through.*

Variety: *Don't be afraid to try new ingredients. We are lucky to have access to a wealth of foods from all over the world, each adding to the texture, flavour and colour of a dish.*

SIMPLE WAYS TO BOOST FLAVOUR

Spices: *Don't underestimate the importance of spices – they can transform your cooking, providing an instant flavour boost. Use them in curry pastes, marinades or spice rubs, or add a little to soups, casseroles or pasta to lift the flavour or add warmth.*

Fresh herbs: *If you have a garden, many herbs are easy to grow at home, or indeed on a sunny windowsill, but if not, most are widely available at your local green grocer or supermarket. Once you get into the habit of using them, it is hard to go back because they really do add an extra dimension to your cooking.*

Hardier herbs, such as bay leaves, rosemary, thyme and sage, are usually added at the beginning of cooking and are excellent for boosting the flavour of many dishes, especially soups, slow-cooked stews, pasta sauces or hearty roasts.

Softer herbs, such as basil, tarragon, parsley, coriander and mint, are usually added at the end of cooking to provide freshness. These softer herbs can also be whizzed into pestos, sauces and dressings or added to salsas and herb butters, which are an easy way to transform plain fish, meat or vegetables from something ordinary into something special.

Lemons and limes: *Often, a squeeze of juice is all that is needed to balance the flavour at the end of cooking. With Asian dishes, in particular, it can be difficult to balance the flavours of salty, sweet and sour, and a little squeeze of citrus juice can help pull everything together.*

Oils and vinegars: *Good-quality oils and vinegars are essential to great-tasting vinaigrettes or dressings; these will make all the difference to a salad. There's no need to spend a fortune: you can get very decent extra-virgin olive oil for salads at a reasonable price. Vinegar is an often under-utilised store-cupboard ingredient, but it is an essential in my kitchen: a splash of vinegar can help balance a sauce or a gravy and it can also be used to make a quick pickle or dipping sauce. I mainly use white wine vinegar. I rarely use nut-flavoured oils as their shelf life is short.*

Wine and spirits: *Midweek, everyday family meals don't call for these, but when you're cooking for a special occasion, a splash of white wine or brandy can transform an ordinary sauce into something more luxurious.*

Condiments: *Like many a cook, I find the number of bottles and jars in my store cupboard just keep on growing! There is such a range of different flavours, all so versatile and extremely handy for enhancing any dish. Whether it's tomato ketchup for adding depth to a casserole or pasta sauce, redcurrant jelly to give a touch of sweetness to a gravy, or horseradish sauce for making a speedy dip, condiments are a brilliant addition to the store cupboard and invaluable to the home cook.*

Seasoning: *Although this is very much down to personal taste, a basic level of seasoning is vital for any savoury dish. If you are cooking from scratch, you will need to add a little salt and pepper to start with, then check the seasoning of the finished dish and add a little more if it needs it, and if in doubt, ask for a second opinion.*

COLOUR, TEXTURE AND PRESENTATION

As the old saying goes, 'We eat with our eyes first', and it's worth taking some time to think about what your finished dish will look like before you begin cooking.

Colour and texture: *Select dishes that complement each other in terms of texture and colour, providing contrast and variety.*

Avoid repetition: *If you have chosen a first course that uses a particular ingredient, such as pastry or cream, for instance, you should avoid pastry or cream in the rest of the menu to ensure that variety is maintained throughout the meal.*

Side dishes: *These should counterbalance the main dish. If your main course has a fairly plain or pale-coloured sauce, for instance, you should choose side salads and vegetables that add some colour to the plate and provide a difference in texture.*

THE FINISHING TOUCHES

Herbs: *If your recipe contains fresh herbs, it can be a good idea to save a few to use as a garnish before serving.*

Cheese: *If your recipe contains cheese, reserve a little to sprinkle or crumble on top of the dish at the end and, if appropriate, brown in the oven or under the grill.*

Black pepper: *A few simple grinds of black pepper can be all that is needed to finish off a dish.*

Dressings and sauces: *Be careful not to drench salad leaves in dressing as this can make the leaves soggy and they will look messy when served. Toss the salad with some of the dressing and, once served, drizzle with a little extra if needed. Similarly, when serving meat with a sauce, place the meat on the plate first, then spoon over the sauce to avoid adding too much.*

PLATING AND SERVING

Plate size: *Take time to decide whether to serve your dish on a plate or in a bowl, and choose the correct size, depending on whether you are serving a starter or main course. When serving a cake, choose the right-sized cake stand or plate so that there is enough room to slice it.*

Presentation: *If there are lots of separate elements in a dish – such as a starter consisting of prawns, quail's eggs, smoked salmon slices, lamb's lettuce and lemon wedges – decide how you are going to present them on the plate before you begin serving.*

Serving: *Be as neat as possible when serving food – serve it slowly and with care.*

RECIPE FINDER

In this collection of recipes, you'll find something to suit every occasion – from weekday family suppers to weekend crowd pleasers and special occasion feasts. I've designed this recipe finder to help you navigate your way through the recipes in this book, making it easier for you to track down exactly what you're looking for.

MAKE EVERY DAY DELICIOUS

When time is short, preparing a nutritious family meal or whipping up dinner for unexpected guests can be challenging. Here you'll find inspiration for the speediest of midweek suppers, prep-ahead crowd pleasers and quick and easy treats.

30-MINUTE MEALS

Quick and flavour-packed, these simple suppers are ideal for midweek cooking and are ready in 30 minutes or less.

Chicken Stir-fry with Teriyaki Sauce 126

Fillet Beef Salad with Asian Dressing 93

Five Spice Salmon Stir-fry 154

Fragrant Light Prawn Curry 155

Fresh and Sun-dried Tomato Pasta with Mozzarella and Basil (V) 171

Griddled Chicken Carbonara 130

Orzo with Broad Beans, Peas, Lemon and Thyme (V) 185

Spaghetti with Courgettes, Tomatoes and Chilli (V) 170

PREP-AHEAD CROWD PLEASERS

These comforting family favourites are perfect for preparing in advance. They take a little bit of time and effort to prepare, yet are very simple to make; indeed, many are slow-cook one-pot dishes that, once on the go, require little attention.

Beef and Ale Stew with Horseradish Spiral Dumplings 87

Homemade Pizza with Parma Ham and Goat's Cheese 99

Chilli con Carne 89

Lamb Fricassee with Pearl Barley 112

Mary's Sausages 97

Melanzane Pasta (V) 180

Potato, Leek and Cheese Pie (V) 186

Ragù Bolognese with Pappardelle 94

Smoked Haddock and Cauliflower Gratin 156

Squash and Black Bean Chilli (V) 179

Tartiflette 205

Venison Cottage Pie 115

Winter Vegetable Soup (V) 62

LOW-PREP WINTER WARMER PUDDINGS

During the chillier months it is lovely to be able to treat family and friends to an occasional pudding, and these are some of my favourite British classics – easy to make and irresistible to eat.

Blackberry and Apple Crumble Pie 235

Classic Rice Pudding 229

Peach Sponge Pudding 230

Pear and Apple Crumble 233

Steamed Golden Apple Pudding 232

Sticky Toffee Pudding 245

EASY TEATIME TREATS

These simple bakes are fairly quick to whip up and involve only simple techniques, so are perfect for less experienced bakers or for making with children.

Ginger and Mango Spiced Muffins 299

Hummingbird Cake 300

Lemon and Pistachio Shortbread Biscuits 292

Mixed Seeded Snaps 291

Orange Oat Cookies 295

Sultana Scones 304

RECIPE FINDER

EXPRESS ENTERTAINING

Our busy lives don't always allow us the luxury of planning ahead, so I've included these recipes for exactly those situations, when you are short of time but keen to make something special for friends or family.

QUICK FIRST COURSES AND NIBBLES	EXPRESS MAINS	EXPRESS MAINS	SUPER-SPEEDY PUDDINGS
Simple, delicious, and easily assembled.	*All of these dishes are ready in 1 hour or less.*	*Continued*	*These puddings can all be prepared in a matter of minutes.*
Beetroot Houmous (V) 52	Crusted Crab and Cod Fillet with Chive Lemon Sauce 159	Spiced Chicken Legs with Roasted Onions 123	Melon and Pineapple Salad with Lime Syrup 250
Thai Crab Poppadom Canapés 34	Fish and Chips with Tartare Sauce 147	Tarragon-Crusted Sea Bass 160	Mojito Cheesecakes 259
Guacamole with Coriander (V) 50	Chicken Breasts with Red Pepper and Goat's Cheese 134	Yuzu Salmon with Buttered Leeks 152	Passion Fruit and Banana Eton Mess 265
Mushroom Bruschetta (V) 68	Chicken Dijon 129		Rosy Fruit Compote with Yoghurt and Honey 273
Individual Smoked Salmon and Prawn Starters with Avocado 75	Chicken Satay Salad 222		Scots Whisky Cream 270
	Chicken, Squash and Fennel Bake 125		
	Chicken Thighs with Garlic Cream Cheese 122		
	Crispy-skinned Duck Breasts with Pak Choi and Pineapple Sauce 138		
	Golden Fried Crab and Basil Spaghetti 164		
	Herb-crusted Lamb Cutlets with Creamy Mint Sauce 108		
	Rack of Lamb with Salsa Verde 107		
	Marsala Mediterranean Chicken Thighs 121		
	Panang Chicken and Rice Stir-fry 133		
	Sea Bream with Samphire and Chives 163		

RECIPE FINDER

MAKE ENTERTAINING EXTRA SPECIAL

Whether you're planning for a celebration, cooking for friends at the weekend or having a family get-together, here are some impressive recipes that you can prepare ahead to make life simpler.

PREP-AHEAD STARTERS AND NIBBLES	PREP-AHEAD MAINS	PREP-AHEAD DESSERTS	FREEZE-AHEAD PUDDINGS	PREP-AHEAD TEATIME TREATS
These are delicious with drinks, and will give you more time with guests.	*Impressive but easy to prepare in advance.*	*These desserts all have a real wow factor.*	*Make a batch for the freezer and you'll always have a homemade dessert on standby for any impromptu guests.*	*These beautiful cakes are perfect for a celebration or a special afternoon tea.*
Artichoke and Garlic Dip (V) 52	Aubergine and Taleggio Bake (V) 183	Apple and Lemon Galette 240	Mango and Passion Fruit Sorbet with Mint Salsa 252	Chocolate Reflection Cake 283
Celeriac Soup with Crispy Pancetta and Poppy Seed Croutons 64	Glazed Ham with Fresh Piccalilli 104	Chocolate and Hazelnut Torte 261	Rhubarb and Ginger Ice Cream 249	Lemon Meringue and Strawberry Cupcakes 279
Curried Beef Samosas 44	Marinated Harissa Prawns with Spiced Rice 151	Fresh Strawberry Tartlets 269		Orange Drizzle Cake 303
Dill, Herring and Quail's Egg Canapés 33	Plum Tomato, Olive and Marjoram Tart (V) 175	Paris–Brest with Double Chocolate 255		Toffee Cupcakes 280
Dough Balls with Garlic Herb Butter (V) 49	Roast Leg of Lamb with a Garlic and Thyme Rub 111	Profiteroles with Warm Chocolate Fudge Sauce 239		Walnut Brittle and Coffee Cake 287
Ginger and Chilli Tiger Prawns with Dipping Sauce 53	Sausage and Herb Plait 103	Rainbow Meringues 266		Weekend Fruitcake 296
Griddled Halloumi with Beetroot Chutney (V) 76	Very Posh Fishcakes 145	White Chocolate and Raspberry Cheesecake 247		
Herbed Blinis with Peas and Pancetta 71				
Jerusalem Artichoke and Celery Soup (V) 63				
Mushroom and Thyme Pâté (V) 79				
Olive Tapenade (V) 39				
Parsnip, Coconut and Lemon Grass Soup 61				
Portobello Mushrooms with Double Cheese Topping (V) 191				
Smoked Haddock and Asparagus Chowder 67				
Smoked Salmon, Red Pepper and Spinach Bites 37				
Spiced Chicken and Chicory Boats 42				
Spicy Mexican Samosas 45				
Sun-blushed Tomato and Basil Tapenade (V) 38				
Three Beetroot Salad with Mozzarella and Basil (V) 218				

MENU PLANS

WINTER WARMER

Winter Vegetable Soup (V) 62

_____

*Beef and Ale Stew with Horseradish
Spiral Dumplings 87*

_____

*Steamed Golden Apple Pudding 232
or
Sticky Toffee Pudding 245*

SUNDAY LUNCH

*Griddled Halloumi with
Beetroot Chutney (V) 76*

_____

*Roast Leg of Lamb with a Garlic
and Thyme Rub 111
with Celeriac and Leek Gratin 197*

_____

Pear and Apple Crumble 233

ITALIAN FEAST FOR A CROWD

*Dough Balls with Garlic
Herb Butter (V) 49*

_____

*Ragù Bolognese with Pappardelle 94
or
Melanzane Pasta (V) 180*

_____

*Profiteroles with Warm
Chocolate Fudge Sauce 239
or
White Chocolate and Raspberry
Cheesecake 247*

MEXICAN WEEKEND FEAST

*Guacamole with Coriander (V) 50
or
Spicy Mexican Samosas 45*

_____

*Squash and Black Bean Chilli (V) 179
or
Chilli con Carne 89*

_____

*Mojito Cheesecakes 259
or
Mango and Passion Fruit Sorbet
with Mint Salsa 252*

MENU PLANS

SPEEDY SUMMER SUPPER

Thai Crab Poppadom Canapés 34
or
Beetroot Houmous (V) 52

_____

*Crispy-skinned Duck Breasts with
Pak Choi and Pineapple Sauce 138*
or
Yuzu Salmon with Buttered Leeks 152
with
*Green Beans and Mangetout with Mint
Caper Butter 202*

_____

Passion Fruit and Banana Eton Mess 265
or
*Rosy Fruit Compote with Yoghurt
and Honey 273*

SPECIAL COLD
CELEBRATION LUNCH

*Dill, Herring and Quail's
Egg Canapés 33*
or
*Smoked Salmon, Red Pepper
and Spinach Bites 37*

_____

Glazed Ham with Fresh Piccalilli 104
with
Celeriac and Tarragon Remoulade 201

_____

Chocolate and Hazelnut Torte 261
or
Apple and Lemon Galette 240

POSH FISH SUPPER FOR FOUR

*Ginger and Chilli Tiger Prawns
with Dipping Sauce 53*

_____

Very Posh Fishcakes 145

_____

Rhubarb and Ginger Ice Cream 249

SPECIAL HOT
CELEBRATION LUNCH

*Celeriac Soup with Crispy Pancetta
and Poppy Seed Croutons 64*
or
Mushroom Bruschetta 68

_____

Rack of Lamb with Salsa Verde 107

_____

Paris Brest with Double Chocolate 255
or
*Rosy Fruit Compote with Yoghurt
and Honey 273*

STORE-CUPBOARD SECRETS

A well-stocked store cupboard and fridge are key to both everyday cooking and entertaining, giving you the flexibility to experiment with new dishes without needing to plan a shopping trip each time you want to try something new. Ensuring you have a wide variety of ingredients at your fingertips will keep you well equipped for exploring new recipes and will ultimately help you become a more adventurous cook. The first step is to stock up on all the basics to make everyday cooking less of an effort. The second step is to invest in a few extra ingredients that will boost flavour and help turn an ordinary dish into something extra special. I like to call these little extras my store-cupboard stars.

I appreciate that it can be tricky deciding which are the most useful items to have to hand, so I've put together this list to help you choose. Eggs (all large in my recipes, unless otherwise stated) are included in the fridge section, but they need to be at room temperature for cake making, so make sure to remove them from the fridge well ahead of time.

Mary's store-cupboard stars

ESSENTIALS FOR A WELL-PREPARED COOK'S STORE CUPBOARD

BAKING	NUTS, SEEDS AND DRIED FRUIT	SPICES, DRIED HERBS AND SEASONINGS
Plain and self-raising flour *Strong flour for bread making* *Semolina* *Baking powder and bicarbonate of soda* *Cornflour* *Cocoa powder* *Ground almonds* *Vanilla extract* *Fast-action dried yeast* *Panko breadcrumbs* *Gelatine powder* **Sugar:** *caster sugar, icing sugar, light muscovado and demerara sugar* *Honey* **Chocolate:** *good-quality white, dark and milk* *Maple syrup* *Golden syrup* *Black treacle* *Digestive and amaretti biscuits*	*Sesame seeds* *Sunflower and pumpkin seeds* *Currants, raisins and sultanas* *Dried apricots* *Dried cranberries, figs, dates and mango*	**Salt:** *table salt and coarse sea salt* *Peppercorns* **Ground spices:** *cumin, coriander, cinnamon, ginger, nutmeg, turmeric, chilli powder, mixed spice, paprika, sweet smoked paprika, black pepper, *cayenne pepper, *za'atar spice blend* **Whole spices:** *nutmeg, cumin, coriander seeds, mustard and fennel seeds, dried chillies, cardamom pods, cinnamon sticks, star anise* **Spice blends:** *garam masala, curry powder, Chinese five spice powder* **Dried herbs:** *bay leaves* **Stock cubes:** *chicken, vegetable and beef*

FOR THE FRIDGE	TINNED AND PRESERVED FOODS	CONDIMENTS AND PRESERVES
Milk	Anchovies in oil	Tomato ketchup
Eggs	Tuna	Tomato purée
Butter	Capers	*Sun-dried tomato paste
Baking spread	Sweet dill-pickled cucumber	*Horseradish sauce
Double cream	Gherkins	Worcestershire sauce
*Cheese: Parmesan, Cheddar, a blue cheese, a goat's cheese and a full-fat cream cheese	Chopped tomatoes	Tabasco sauce
	Passata	Sweet chilli sauce
	Chickpeas	Soy sauce
*Crème fraîche	*Sweetcorn	*Hoisin sauce
*Greek-style yoghurt	Beans: butter beans, cannellini beans, kidney beans, *flageolet beans, *borlotti beans	Thai fish sauce
*Streaky bacon or pancetta		Thai curry paste
*Puff pastry		*Harissa paste
	Olives	*Tamarind paste
	Ready-roasted peppers	*Pomegranate molasses
	Coconut milk	**Jams:** apricot, strawberry, raspberry, marmalade and lemon curd
	*Full-fat condensed milk	
	Sun-dried tomatoes	Redcurrant jelly
	*Sun-blushed tomatoes	*Caramelised onion marmalade
	*Dried porcini mushrooms	*Mango chutney
	*Preserved lemons	*Stem ginger in syrup
		*Peanut butter
		Good-quality mayonnaise
		Mustard: English, Dijon, wholegrain and powdered

WINE AND SPIRITS FOR COOKING	DRIED GRAINS AND PULSES	PASTA, NOODLES AND RICE	OILS AND VINEGARS
White and red wine	Rolled oats	Linguine or spaghetti	Olive oil and extra-virgin olive oil
*Ale	Couscous	Penne and other pasta shapes	Sunflower oil
*Marsala wine or dry white sherry	*Quinoa	Lasagne sheets	Sesame oil
*Sweet sherry	*Bulgar wheat	Orzo	*Flavoured oils
*Brandy	*Pearl barley	Egg noodles	White wine vinegar
*Rum	Lentils (red and Puy)	*Rice noodles	Balsamic vinegar
		Rice: basmati (white or brown), risotto and pudding rice, *jasmine and *wild rice, parboiled rice	Rice vinegar

HOW TO MAKE THE MOST
OF YOUR FREEZER

Making full use of your freezer can ease the pressure when it comes to both everyday cooking and one-off entertaining. For everyday cooking, it can act as an extension of your store cupboard – ideal for keeping handy basics as well as helping to reduce waste by enabling you to freeze and store leftover portions of cooked dishes and fresh ingredients that you can't use immediately. The freezer can also be a godsend when you have guests. If you are planning a party or celebratory meal, it enables you to make everything ahead of time, from starters and main courses to desserts and cakes, leaving you less cooking to do at the last minute. See below for some tips on freezing different kinds of food – what freezes well and what doesn't – and how best to organise your freezer.

EVERYDAY COOKING

Ready-frozen vegetables *are a brilliant standby and will help you stick to a healthy diet even when time is short. I always keep a bag of petits pois in the freezer to serve either on their own or with sautéed courgettes or leeks.*

Most fresh vegetables *can be frozen (except those with a particularly high water content – see page 27). Before freezing, blanch in boiling water for 1–3 minutes, then drain and plunge straight into ice-cold water to halt the cooking process. Frozen vegetables (blanched or ready-frozen) should be cooked from frozen, rather than defrosted first.*

Most herbs *can be frozen: chop and freeze in ice-cube trays topped up with a little water. Softer herbs like tarragon and basil are better made into a pesto or a herb butter before freezing (see also page 27).*

Ginger, chilli and garlic *Knobs of fresh root ginger can be frozen: simply wrap in cling film and grate from frozen. Chillies should be chopped before freezing; they can also be used straight from the freezer as they will defrost almost instantly. Peel garlic cloves before freezing, wrap really well and then grate straight from frozen.*

Curry leaves, kaffir lime leaves and bay leaves *can all be frozen and are useful to have in the freezer for adding authentic flavour to curries, soups and casseroles.*

Most fresh fruit *freezes very well and is excellent to have on standby for making an impromptu pud. Berries such as raspberries, blackberries, redcurrants and blueberries should be frozen in a single layer on a tray until solid and then decanted into a freezer bag; this will prevent them from being squashed or damaged. Soft fruits such as strawberries and peaches will turn mushy on freezing and discolour once halved, so it's best to purée them first. Apples, rhubarb, plums and cherries are best stewed with a little sugar before freezing.*

Nuts *can be stored in the freezer, including almonds (whole, blanched, ground and flaked), coconut (desiccated and flaked), pistachios, hazelnuts, pine nuts and salted peanuts.*

Raw meat and fish *freeze well. Always make sure it is as fresh as possible, wrap really well and, as a general rule, don't keep it for longer than 3 months – see also page 26.*

Cooked meat *can also be frozen. Ensure it is completely cold before freezing.*

Milk *It is handy to keep a pint of full-fat or semi-skimmed milk in the freezer; defrost in a sink of cold water and shake well before use.*

Cream *Double cream and clotted cream freeze well because of their high fat content – freeze for up to 3 months.*

Butter and hard cheese *(such as Parmesan and Cheddar) can be frozen. It's useful to grate hard cheese before freezing as this will defrost more quickly.*

Eggs *Raw egg whites and yolks can be frozen separately. This is really useful if you have made a meringue or custard and have some separated egg whites or yolks left over. Ensure you make a note of the quantity on the label.*

Bread *freezes very well and is an essential standby. Ready-sliced bread can be toasted straight from frozen. Allow a couple of hours for whole loaves of bread to defrost.*

ENTERTAINING

Whether you're planning a birthday celebration, a dinner party or Christmas lunch, getting ahead by freezing starters, main courses, desserts and cakes can be invaluable.

First and main courses *Many cooked and cooled dishes – such as soups, casseroles, bakes, gratins and fishcakes – can be frozen. I often double up a recipe when I'm cooking in order to have one to eat straight away and one to freeze for a later date.*

Hot and cold puddings *Meringues, cheesecakes and pastry-based desserts are among those that can be frozen – always refer to the recipe for how best to do this. In general, it's best to open-freeze until solid in order to prevent damage, then wrap well and freeze until needed.*

Cakes, biscuits and pastry

Raw cookie and biscuit dough can be frozen in a log shape; defrost, then slice into rounds to bake.

It's often easier to freeze a made-up raw pastry case rather than a block of pastry. Pastry cases that have been baked blind can also be frozen, but they can become more fragile to handle.

Non-iced cakes can be frozen. Ensure the sponges are completely cold, then wrap in a double layer of cling film to protect against freezer burn. Allow 3–4 hours to defrost at room temperature, depending on the size of the cake.

Baked biscuits and cookies can be frozen. Before freezing, make sure they are packed snugly into a freezer-proof container, in layers of kitchen paper, to reduce the amount of air surrounding them.

HOW TO ORGANISE YOUR FREEZER

Label and date *everything that goes into the freezer. This will not only make it easier to find what you're looking for, but you'll be less likely to forget what you have or risk keeping it in the freezer too long. Write down the number of servings, together with any reheating instructions and other short notes.*

Group foods together: *Aim to keep the same types of foods together by allocating them to different shelves or drawers. Keep meat and fish in one drawer, for instance, and cakes, biscuits and puddings together in another drawer.*

Keep a list *of exactly what is in the freezer and the date when it was frozen. This will help you to keep tabs on what needs using up; it will also make meal planning easier if you're aware of what you already have. Make sure you keep it up to date by crossing things off the list when you have used them.*

Don't freeze cooked dishes for longer than 3 months *Many foods will keep in the freezer for up to 6 months, and some – such as fresh vegetables, large joints of meat and game – can be frozen for up to a year. However, the flavour and quality of the food will deteriorate over time, so it's best to keep track of how long things have been frozen so that you can enjoy them at their best. Aim to tidy your freezer every 2 months so that you can see what needs to be used up. Gather these items together in a box or container to remind you when you open the freezer.*

HOW TO PREPARE FOOD FOR THE FREEZER

Ensure food is cold *Cooked food needs to be completely cold before it can be frozen, to ensure food safety.*

Double-wrap food to protect against freezer burn *Freezing can be harsh on certain foods, so double-wrap in foil or cling film or use resealable freezer bags to help prevent foods from being damaged.*

Leave space for expansion of liquids *Don't forget that liquids expand on freezing, so take care not to fill containers or freezer bags all the way to the top when adding soups, stocks or purées. Leave a little space to allow room for the liquid to expand.*

Use the correct size of container *When freezing cooked solid food or leftovers, it's important to decant it into an appropriate-sized freezer-proof container to ensure minimal air surrounds the food; too much space (i.e. air) around the food will cause it to dry out during freezing. If using freezer bags, ensure that you squeeze out as much air as possible.*

Don't freeze food which is past its best *If you're freezing something because you don't want to waste it but you know it's no longer fresh, it really isn't worth the freezer space as it won't improve on freezing.*

HOW TO DEFROST AND REHEAT FOOD SAFELY

Defrost in a cool place *Ideally all food (especially meat and fish) should be defrosted slowly in the fridge overnight. This is less important for breads, cakes and biscuits, which can be thawed at room temperature.*

Allow plenty of time *Large joints of meat and a whole turkey can take up to 2 days to defrost thoroughly, so ensure you plan ahead*

Use the microwave *Most microwaves have a defrost function that enables you to defrost food safely and quickly; follow your instruction manual for the best results.*

Reheat thoroughly *To avoid any risk of food poisoning, it is crucial that meat, fish and poultry dishes are fully reheated until piping hot all the way through. They should be cooked on the hob or in the oven until they reach boiling point in the centre for 5 minutes (or 3–4 minutes in the microwave).*

Don't try to speed up *or rush the thawing process. Not only does this carry a risk of food poisoning, but the texture of the food may be adversely affected.*

FOODS THAT ARE BEST NOT FROZEN

Salad ingredients *The water content of most salad ingredients (such as tomatoes, lettuce and cucumber) is too high for successful freezing; they would turn mushy on defrosting.*

Fresh, soft herbs *(such as basil, coriander and dill) are too delicate to freeze as they are, but you can whizz them into a pesto or make a herb butter (by adding them to softened butter) before freezing.*

Low-fat dairy products *(such as yoghurt, single cream and cream cheese) turn watery and separate on defrosting.*

Egg-based sauces *(such as hollandaise or mayonnaise) cannot be frozen as they will separate on defrosting.*

Cooked eggs *do not freeze well; they become rubbery in texture.*

Cooked vegetables *(such as peas and leeks) become watery on thawing.*

Previously frozen meat or fish *can't be frozen again in a raw state, but if it is carefully defrosted and then cooked (for example, in a pie or casserole), it can be frozen.*

FOOD FOR
SHARING

It's always a pleasure to cook for a crowd, and it needn't be stressful or excessively time consuming. I've gathered a selection of recipes which will suit more formal occasions or relaxed drinks with friends and family. Moreish Artichoke and Garlic Dip (page 52) will be snapped up very quickly, or my Smoked Salmon, Red Pepper and Spinach Bites (page 37) are perfect drinks party nibbles.

DILL, HERRING AND QUAIL'S EGG CANAPÉS

These tasty little morsels are perfect for any special occasion. Quail's eggs and jars of herrings marinated in dill are available from some supermarkets and delicatessens. You can buy quail's eggs ready-boiled, too, if you need to save time. Rye bread is firm with a lovely nutty flavour and texture – ideal for a canapé as it does not go soggy quickly.

MAKES 24 CANAPÉS

COOK TIME:
3 MINUTES

6 quail's eggs

4 small slices of rye bread (see tip)

100g (4oz) cream cheese

1 tsp lemon juice

1 tbsp chopped dill, plus sprigs of dill to garnish

50g (2oz) herrings in dill marinade from a jar (drained weight), cut into small squares

Freshly ground black pepper

1. To hard-boil the quail's eggs, place in a saucepan of boiling water and cook for 3 minutes, then plunge into cold water to cool them quickly, changing the water again as it warms up. (This should keep the egg yolks bright and yellow with no grey-blue ring around the cooked yolk.) Peel the eggs as soon as they are cold (see tip).

2. Cut each slice of bread into six small squares and arrange on a long plate or board.

3. Place the cream cheese, lemon juice and dill in a bowl, season with pepper and mix until combined. Spread a thin layer over each square of bread. Sit a piece of herring on top of each square and blob the remaining mixture on top of the herring.

4. Slice each hard-boiled quail's egg into quarters. Place a quarter on top of each piece of herring and garnish with a sprig of dill.

PREPARE AHEAD

Can be assembled up to 2 hours ahead.

MARY'S EVERYDAY TIPS

Slices of leftover rye bread from the loaf can be topped with smoked salmon to serve as another canapé.

It's best to peel the cooled quail's eggs immediately as the membrane around the egg comes away more easily.

THAI CRAB POPPADOM CANAPÉS

These are such quick canapés to make. You can buy mini poppadoms in a packet, as you would crisps, but otherwise mini croustade cases would make a good alternative. Tinned crabmeat is actually just as good as fresh for this recipe as it needs to be finely shredded; indeed, larger pieces would be a bit too big for topping the poppadoms.

MAKES 15 CANAPÉS

PREP TIME:
5–10 MINUTES, PLUS
MARINATING

100g (4oz) white crabmeat
  (tinned or fresh – see tip)
½ fresh red chilli, deseeded
  and finely chopped
About 1 tsp mayonnaise
1 tsp sweet chilli
  dipping sauce
Squeeze of lime juice
15 mini poppadoms
Salt and freshly ground
  black pepper
Fresh coriander leaves,
  to garnish

1. Squeeze out any excess liquid from the crabmeat in a sieve lined with kitchen paper then add the crabmeat to a bowl with the chilli, mayonnaise, chilli sauce and lime juice. Season with salt and pepper and stir to combine until the consistency is soft. Set aside for a minimum of 30 minutes for the flavours to blend.

2. When ready to serve, spoon a teaspoon of the crab mixture into each poppadom and garnish with a small coriander leaf. Serve at once to prevent the poppadoms from going soggy (see tip).

PREPARE AHEAD

The crab mixture can be made up to a day ahead and kept in the fridge.

MARY'S EVERYDAY TIPS

If buying fresh crabmeat, watch out for any little pieces of bone or shell that may have been left in the meat – you might want to pick it over first before using.

These canapés will hold for about 30 minutes before going soggy. It's therefore best to add the topping at the last minute, or better still – ask a helpful guest!

SMOKED SALMON, RED PEPPER AND SPINACH BITES

These are great as a canapé as one quantity of the recipe makes 50 bites – perfect for a crowd. The base is my twist on a spinach roulade; filled with tangy cream cheese and topped with a sliver of salmon or roasted red pepper, the assembled canapés are colourful, light and full of flavour.

MAKES 50 CANAPÉS

COOK TIME:
12 MINUTES, PLUS COOLING

100g (4oz) baby spinach

4 eggs, separated

100g (4oz) cream cheese

1 tbsp creamed horseradish sauce from a jar

1 tbsp snipped chives

Salt and freshly ground black pepper

FOR THE TOPPING

100g (4oz) smoked salmon slices or trimmings (see introduction), cut into 25 small slices

100g (4oz) roasted red peppers from a jar, cut into 25 small slices

1. You will need a 23 x 30cm (9 x 12in) Swiss roll/roulade tin and a piping bag fitted with a plain nozzle. Preheat the oven to 200°C/180°C fan/Gas 6 and line the tin with baking paper.

2. Whizz the spinach in a food processor until finely chopped. Add the egg yolks, season with salt and pepper and whizz for 10 seconds. Tip into a bowl.

3. Whisk the egg whites with an electric hand whisk in a spotlessly clean bowl until forming stiff peaks. Carefully fold into the spinach mixture and then spoon into the prepared tin, levelling the top.

4. Bake in the oven for about 12 minutes or until puffed up and just firm on top. Set aside to cool for 10 minutes. Lay a sheet of baking paper on a worktop, then tip the tin over to invert the cooked spinach roulade on to the paper and carefully remove the lining paper. Leave to cool down completely.

5. Slice the roulade in half widthways. Measure the cream cheese, horseradish and chives into a bowl, season with salt and pepper and mix. Spoon half of this mixture on to one half of the spinach roulade, spreading right to the edges. Sit the other half on top to make a sandwich measuring 15 x 23cm (6 x 9in).

6. Use a serrated knife (see tip) to slice into 50 tiny 'squares' by dividing the sandwich into five at 3cm (1¼in) intervals along the short edge and ten at 2.3cm (1in) intervals along the long edge. Put the remaining cream cheese mixture into the piping bag, then pipe a small blob on top of each square.

7. Top the canapés with pieces of pepper and chopped salmon. Arrange on a platter with a cocktail stick speared through each one, if you like, to hold everything together and make it easier to eat.

PREPARE AHEAD

Can be assembled up to 4 hours ahead.

MARY'S EVERYDAY TIP

A serrated knife keeps the edges clean and prevents them from being squashed as you cut through the layers of the sandwich.

SUN-BLUSHED TOMATO AND BASIL TAPENADE

The sun-blushed tomatoes give this tapenade a wonderfully intense flavour. Great to have in the fridge to use on a canapé or as a spread or dip – you name it!

MAKES 250G (9OZ)

PREP TIME: 5 MINUTES

200g (7oz) sun-blushed
  tomatoes (see tip on
  page 170)

1 handful of basil leaves

1 garlic clove, peeled

2 tbsp good olive oil (see tip)

50g (2oz) pine nuts

Put all the ingredients into a food processor and whizz until smooth. Use straight away or store in an airtight container in the fridge.

PREPARE AHEAD

Will keep in the fridge for up to a week.

MARY'S EVERYDAY TIP

For extra flavour, replace the olive oil with some of the oil from the tub of sun-blushed tomatoes.

OLIVE TAPENADE

Like the Sun-blushed Tomato and Basil Tapenade on page 38, this is great to have in the fridge to use as a dip or spread on a canapé. Buy the best olives you can afford, preferably in oil, rather than brine, as they have more flavour.

MAKES 230G (8OZ)

PREP TIME: 5 MINUTES

100g (4oz) pitted black olives (drained weight)

100g (4oz) pitted green olives (drained weight)

2 tbsp olive oil (reserved from the jar if using olives in oil)

2 anchovies in oil, drained

½ garlic clove, peeled (see tip)

Freshly ground black pepper

1. Put all the ingredients into a food processor, seasoning with black pepper (the olives and anchovies provide enough salt). Whizz until as smooth as possible, stopping every now and then to scrape down the sides of the processor bowl with a spatula so that all the mixture is incorporated.

2. Use straight away or store in an airtight container in the fridge (see tip).

PREPARE AHEAD

Will keep in the fridge for 1–2 weeks.

MARY'S EVERYDAY TIPS

Crush the garlic clove with the back of a knife to make it easier to peel.

Cover the tapenade with a layer of oil to store and to help prevent air getting to it.

SPICED CHICKEN AND CHICORY BOATS

Spicy chicken served on a crisp cool base, these would be great for a first course or a light summer lunch. It's best to use red chicory for its lovely colour, but green chicory would taste just as good. If you are not keen on chicory, wrap the filling in iceberg or Little Gem leaves instead. For a proper sharing dish and a more relaxed meal, you could arrange the leaves, mayonnaise and chicken in separate dishes for your guests to top or wrap their own.

MAKES 12 CANAPÉS / SERVES 4 AS A STARTER, OR LIGHT LUNCH WITH A FEW SALAD LEAVES

COOK TIME:
5–6 MINUTES

1 tbsp oil

350g (12oz) skinless and boneless chicken breast, very finely chopped (see tip)

1 spring onion, finely chopped, keeping white and green parts separate

1 fresh red chilli, deseeded and finely chopped

2cm (¾in) knob of fresh root ginger, peeled and finely grated (see tip on page 61)

2 tbsp hoisin sauce

12 chicory leaves or small lettuce leaves (iceberg or Little Gem)

About 60ml (2fl oz) mayonnaise

Salt and freshly ground black pepper

1. Heat the oil in a frying pan, then season the chopped chicken with salt and pepper and fry over a high heat for 2–4 minutes until golden all over.

2. Add the white parts of the spring onion to the pan with the chilli and ginger and fry for 2 minutes. Stir in the hoisin sauce to coat the chicken, and season with salt and pepper. (As the hoisin sauce is salty, you won't need to add much salt.)

3. To serve, arrange the chicory or lettuce leaves on a long plate or board, spread about 1 teaspoon of the mayonnaise in the base of each leaf and top with a spoonful of the hot chicken mixture (see tip). Garnish with the green parts of the spring onion and serve either hot or cold.

PREPARE AHEAD

The chicken can be cooked up to a day ahead and pan-fried to serve hot.

If serving cold, the chicory cups can be assembled up to an hour ahead; the lettuce wraps can be made up to 30 minutes ahead.

MARY'S EVERYDAY TIPS

For very fine pieces, you could chop the chicken breasts briefly in a food processor, but be careful not to overdo it. For speed you could buy chicken mince, or ask your butcher to mince some chicken breast for you.

If serving this dish hot, and to speed things up, you may prefer to add the mayonnaise to the leaves while the chicken is still cooking and then add the chicken as soon as it is cooked.

CURRIED BEEF SAMOSAS

With their delicious spicy filling and crispy texture, these are guaranteed to go down well. Perfect for sharing, either as a canapé or a starter.

**MAKES 14
LARGE SAMOSAS**

**COOK TIME:
35 MINUTES, PLUS
COOLING**

1 tbsp sunflower oil

1 onion, finely chopped

½ red pepper, deseeded
and diced

½ fresh red chilli, deseeded
and finely chopped

1 carrot, peeled and
finely diced

2cm (¾in) knob of fresh root
ginger, peeled and finely
grated (see tip on page 61)

300g (11oz) lean minced beef

1–2 tbsp medium
curry powder

1 x 400g tin of chopped
tomatoes

1 tbsp mango chutney

75g (3oz) petits pois
(defrosted if frozen)

7 sheets of filo pastry

Butter, melted, for brushing

1. Heat the oil in a large frying pan, add the onion, red pepper, chilli, carrot and ginger and fry over a high heat for about 2 minutes. Add the beef and fry with the vegetables until browned.

2. Sprinkle in the curry powder, add the tomatoes and mango chutney and season with salt and pepper. Give everything a good stir and bring to the boil. Cover with a lid, lower the heat and simmer for about 10 minutes. Remove the lid, and continue to cook to drive off any liquid, so the mixture is fairly dry. Add the peas and toss together, then set aside to cool for 15 minutes.

3. Meanwhile, preheat the oven to 200°C/180°C fan/Gas 6.

4. Lay a sheet of filo pastry on a board and brush with some of the melted butter. Place another sheet on top, brush with more melted butter and then use a sharp knife to cut the filo sheets into four thin strips lengthways (see tips).

5. Put a tablespoonful of mixture at the top of one strip. Fold over diagonally to form a triangle and continue to fold until you have a neat triangular parcel. Repeat with the remaining sheets and filling, to give 14 parcels. (Cut the seventh filo sheet in half and sandwich both halves together, then divide into two strips to make two parcels.) Brush all over with melted butter.

6. Arrange on a large baking sheet and bake for 15–18 minutes or until golden and very crisp. Serve hot.

PREPARE AHEAD

Can be made up to a day ahead and reheated to crisp up.

MARY'S EVERYDAY TIPS

Sheets of filo pastry tend to vary in size. To make each samosa, you need a long thin strip about 10 x 40cm (4 x 16in). You can make smaller, canapé-sized samosas with strips cut to half the size and half the filling.

The pastry dries out quickly, making it harder to work with. Keep it covered with a clean damp tea towel – removing one sheet at a time, then re-covering it.

SPICY MEXICAN SAMOSAS

I've given these samosas a Mexican twist by filling them with chicken spiced with cumin, coriander and smoked paprika and mixed with a good sprinkling of grated cheese. Like the Curried Beef Samosas on page 44, these will go down a treat with your guests, whether as a canapé or starter.

MAKES 14 SAMOSAS

COOK TIME:
25 MINUTES, PLUS
COOLING

1 tbsp sunflower oil

1 large onion, chopped

½ red pepper, deseeded
and diced

2 garlic cloves, crushed

2 skinless and boneless
chicken breasts, sliced
into thin strips

2 tsp runny honey

1 tsp ground cumin

1 tsp ground coriander

½ heaped tsp sweet
smoked paprika

Juice of ½ lime

3 tomatoes, deseeded and
roughly chopped

1 tbsp chopped coriander

50g (2oz) Cheddar
cheese, grated

7 sheets of filo pastry

Butter, melted, for brushing

1. Preheat the oven to 200°C/180°C fan/Gas 6.

2. Heat the oil in a large frying pan, add the onion, red pepper and garlic and fry over a medium heat for 3–4 minutes. Add the chicken, raise the heat and fry for about 3 minutes until golden all over, then pour over the honey. Sprinkle in the spices, stir well and add the lime juice and tomatoes before frying for another minute.

3. Remove from the heat and stir in the chopped coriander. Tip into a food processor and whizz for 1 minute until roughly chopped (see tip). Transfer to a bowl to cool, then stir in the cheese.

4. Lay a sheet of filo pastry on a board and brush with some of the melted butter. Place another sheet on top, brush with more melted butter and then use a sharp knife to cut the filo sheets into four thin strips lengthways (see tips on page 44).

5. Put a tablespoonful of mixture at the top of one strip. Fold over diagonally to form a triangle and continue to fold until you have a neat triangular parcel. Repeat with the remaining sheets and filling, to give 14 parcels. (Cut the seventh filo sheet in half and sandwich both halves together, then divide into two strips to make two parcels.) Brush all over with melted butter.

6. Arrange on a large baking sheet and bake for 15–18 minutes or until golden and very crisp. Serve hot.

PREPARE AHEAD

Can be made up to a day ahead and reheated to crisp up.

MARY'S EVERYDAY TIP

Cooking the filling mixture first and then processing it keeps the moisture in the chicken.

DOUGH BALLS WITH GARLIC HERB BUTTER

Everyone loves to buy dough balls when they're eating out and this is a quick way to make them at home. They're so versatile too – enjoy them on the side with a pasta dish, or with a topping as a canapé or starter. This recipe makes 20 fairly large-sized balls, but you could easily make 40 smaller ones, if you preferred.

MAKES 20 DOUGH BALLS

COOK TIME:
15–18 MINUTES, PLUS RISING

325g (11oz) strong white flour, plus extra for dusting

7g fast-action dried yeast (see tip on page 100)

2 tbsp olive oil, plus extra for greasing

250ml (9fl oz) lukewarm water

Salt

FOR THE GARLIC HERB BUTTER

100g (4oz) butter, softened

2 garlic cloves, crushed

1 handful of parsley, finely chopped

1. You will need a 25 x 30cm (10 x 12in) roasting tin, well greased with oil.

2. Measure the flour, yeast and olive oil into a large bowl. Add 1 teaspoon of salt to a separate part of the bowl from the yeast (see tip) and stir in the warm water. Mix to combine, then bring together with your hands into a ball.

3. Transfer the dough to a worktop dusted with flour and knead for 5–10 minutes until smooth. Place in a large oiled bowl, cover with cling film and leave to rise or prove in a warm place for 1–1½ hours or until doubled in size.

4. Meanwhile, make the herb butter by placing the butter, garlic and parsley in a bowl and mixing together.

5. Once the dough has doubled in size, tip on to a floured work surface and knead again – this is known as knocking back. Divide into 20 even-sized balls and arrange in the roasting tin in rows of four across and five down, so they are just touching. Cover with cling film and leave to rise again or prove in a warm place for 30–45 minutes.

6. Meanwhile, preheat the oven to 220°C/200°C fan/Gas 7. Bake the dough balls in the oven for 15–18 minutes until golden, well risen and cooked through.

7. Remove from the oven and, using a pastry brush, spread the herb butter over the dough balls. Alternatively, just dip the hot bread into the soft butter.

PREPARE AHEAD

Keep the dough balls in the fridge to prove more slowly, and take out to finish rising before cooking. Or the dough can be made and stored overnight in the fridge, then shaped the following day.

The herb butter can be made 1–2 days in advance and kept in the fridge.

MARY'S EVERYDAY TIPS

When measuring the ingredients into the bowl, it's important to keep the salt and yeast on separate sides of the bowl so the salt doesn't kill the yeast and therefore stop it working.

The butter can be put into small ramekins for individual servings.

GUACAMOLE WITH CORIANDER

Two types of avocado are readily available – Fuerte and Hass. Hass are the more knobbly-skinned variety with a creamier flesh, while Fuerte have a smoother skin and are slightly more watery. Either would work well in this recipe, so long as they are ripe enough (see tip). I like to serve guacamole with a slightly chunkier texture than the kind you buy in shops, but it's entirely up to you – if you like it smooth, whizz for longer. Delicious served with toasted pitta bread, crudités or with my Squash and Black Bean Chilli (see page 179).

**SERVES 6–8 AS
A DIP OR SPREAD**

PREP TIME:
10 MINUTES

1 medium tomato, quartered

2 just-ripe avocados (see tip),
   peeled and chopped

1 fresh green chilli, deseeded
   and chopped

1 garlic clove, crushed

2 heaped tbsp chopped
   coriander

Juice and finely grated
   zest of ½ lime

Salt and freshly ground
   black pepper

1. Scoop the seeds out of the tomato quarters and discard, then roughly chop the flesh. Add to a food processor with the other ingredients and season with salt and pepper. Whizz until finely chopped but still with a little texture.

2. Taste and add more seasoning if you like, then transfer to a bowl (see tip) and either use straight away or store, covered, in the fridge.

PREPARE AHEAD

Can be made up to a day ahead and kept stored in the fridge.

MARY'S EVERYDAY TIPS

The avocados should yield to gentle pressure when they are ripe. If your avocados haven't ripened fully, put them in a bag with a banana. The gases emitted from the banana as it ripens will ripen the avocados too.

Place a stone from one of the avocados in the bowl of the guacamole. This and the lime juice will help prevent it discolouring.

ARTICHOKE AND GARLIC DIP

This is so delicious and quick to make that it will become a real favourite. It's great for entertaining – serve with toasted sourdough, tortilla crisps or crudités. Once you start eating, you'll find it hard to stop!

SERVES 20 AS A DIP

PREP TIME:
5–10 MINUTES

200g (7oz) low-fat
  mayonnaise

150g (5oz) soured cream

100g (4oz) mature Cheddar
  cheese, finely grated

25g (1oz) Parmesan cheese,
  finely grated

¼ small onion, roughly
  chopped

1–2 garlic cloves, grated

1 x 400g tin of artichoke
  hearts (see tip), drained

Salt and freshly ground
  black pepper

Snipped chives, to garnish

1. Measure the mayonnaise and soured cream into a food processor, then add the two cheeses with the onion, garlic and artichokes. Season with salt and pepper and whizz until blended.

2. Check the seasoning, adding more salt and pepper if needed, and spoon into a bowl. Sprinkle with a few snipped chives to serve.

PREPARE AHEAD

Can be made up to 2 days ahead and kept in the fridge, but bear in mind that the garlic flavour will get stronger the longer it infuses.

MARY'S EVERYDAY TIP

Artichoke hearts preserved in oil would do just as well here. Whether from a tin or a jar, they need to be well drained before using; if they are too wet, they will make the dip runny and watery. After draining the artichokes, empty into a bowl and give each one an extra squeeze to release the liquid inside.

BEETROOT HOUMOUS

Bright in both colour and flavour, this is wonderful served as a dip with crudités or on small slices of toasted bread as crostini. If you prefer less garlic, just put in two cloves instead of three. Use a vacuum pack of ready-cooked beetroot if you haven't got fresh.

**SERVES 20 AS
A DIP OR SPREAD**

PREP TIME: 10 MINUTES

300g (11oz) cooked beetroot.
  peeled

1 x 400g tin of chickpeas,
  drained and rinsed (see tip)

3 garlic cloves, sliced

1 tbsp ground cumin

Juice of 1 lemon

120ml (4fl oz) good
  olive oil (see tip)

Salt and freshly ground
  black pepper

Place all the ingredients in a food processor, season with salt and pepper and whizz until smooth. Check the seasoning and transfer to a bowl for serving.

PREPARE AHEAD

Can be made up to a day ahead.

MARY'S EVERYDAY TIPS

The chickpeas need to be well drained so that they don't add extra liquid to the blended mix.

Use good olive oil to add to the flavour of this dip. Sunflower or vegetable oil will not have a strong enough taste.

GINGER AND CHILLI TIGER PRAWNS WITH DIPPING SAUCE

These are great to serve as a canapé, to hand around for your guests to pick up and dip into the sweet sauce. Good as a starter too – serve three sticks per person with rocket leaves.

MAKES 12 CANAPÉS / SERVES 4 AS A STARTER

PREP TIME:
10 MINUTES, PLUS MARINATING

24 cooked tiger prawns (1 x 200g packet), peeled

Salt and freshly ground black pepper

FOR THE MARINADE AND DIPPING SAUCE

Juice of 1 lime (see tip)

2 tbsp good olive oil

1 tsp finely grated fresh root ginger (see tip on page 61)

1 tbsp finely chopped coriander

3 tbsp sweet chilli sauce

1 tbsp soy sauce

1. You will need 12 cocktail sticks (see tip).

2. To make the marinade, measure the ingredients into a bowl and mix together to combine. Add the prawns, season with salt and pepper and leave to marinate for a minimum of 30 minutes.

3. Thread two marinated prawns on each cocktail stick. Arrange on a plate or dish and drizzle over some of the marinade. Pour the remainder into a small dipping dish and place next to the prawns to serve.

PREPARE AHEAD

The prawns can be left to marinate up to a day ahead.

The sauce can be made up to 4 days ahead.

MARY'S EVERYDAY TIPS

To get the most juice out of a hard lime, roll it between your hands, or on a work surface, for a minute before juicing. The lime will become softer and it'll be easier to squeeze out its juice.

The dish is as much about presentation as it is about flavour, and the cocktail sticks are an integral part of this. Many very attractive kinds are available to buy and will help make these canapés look extra-special.

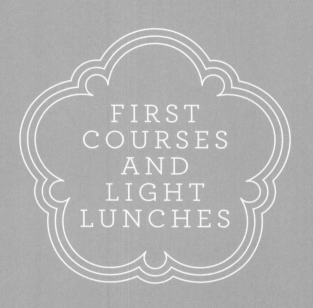

FIRST
COURSES
AND
LIGHT
LUNCHES

The trick with first
courses is to choose something
you can assemble quickly and easily,
or prepare ahead, allowing you to spend
more time with your guests. Celeriac
Soup with Crispy Pancetta and Poppy
Seed Croutons (page 64) is simple
and delicious but substantial enough
to satisfy as a light lunch, or try my
Two-sided Herbed Smoked Salmon and
Horseradish Pâté (page 72).

PARSNIP, COCONUT AND LEMON GRASS SOUP

Slightly different, this soup has a deliciously smooth creamy taste with a hint of ginger and the Orient. Bashing the lemon grass encourages the flavours to infuse the soup. Thai basil has small narrow leaves, purple stems and pink-purple flowers, and is slightly hardier than its Mediterranean cousin. Its distinctive aroma is perfect for this dish, but coriander would work well too.

SERVES 6 (MAKES 1.75 LITRES / 3 PINTS)

COOK TIME: 25 MINUTES

1 tbsp sunflower oil

750g (1lb 10oz) parsnips, peeled and cut into 2cm (¾in) chunks

1 onion, finely chopped

5cm (2in) knob of fresh root ginger, peeled and grated (see tip)

1 tbsp Thai red curry paste

2 tsp runny honey

1 x 400g tin of full-fat coconut milk (see tip)

450ml (15fl oz) vegetable stock

1 tbsp Thai fish sauce

1 lemon grass stalk, kept whole, bashed to bruise

Thai basil or coriander leaves, to garnish

1. Heat the oil in a large saucepan. Tip in the parsnips and onion, and fry over a high heat for a 3–4 minutes until starting to brown. Add the ginger, red curry paste and honey and fry for 30 seconds, then add the coconut milk, stock, fish sauce and lemon grass.

2. Bring to the boil, then cover with a lid, reduce the heat and simmer for about 15 minutes or until the vegetables are tender and soft. Check the seasoning, adding salt and pepper to taste, then remove the lemon grass and discard.

3. Remove from the heat and whizz until smooth, either using a hand blender or in a free-standing blender or food processor.

4. Serve in warmed soup bowls scattered with Thai basil or coriander.

PREPARE AHEAD

Can be made up to 2 days ahead.

FREEZE *Freezes well.*

MARY'S EVERYDAY TIPS

Any leftover ginger from a larger piece can be frozen until needed again. Keep a stock in the freezer so it's always to hand, and grate straight from frozen. Grate across the grain for the best results.

Full-fat coconut milk gives a good consistency to the soup; the low-fat kind may cause the soup to split. Shake the can well before using.

WINTER VEGETABLE SOUP

Made with a range of vegetables, this is a wonderfully comforting soup and so good for you too. It's also great for using up any vegetables that have been hanging around a bit too long, such as yellowing celery and old carrots. You can use the whole of the celery plant for this recipe, chopping up the leaves and central core with the stalks.

SERVES 6

COOK TIME:
30 MINUTES

25g (1oz) butter

1 tbsp olive oil

400g (14oz) leeks (about 2 medium), thinly sliced

400g (14oz) celery sticks (about 2), thinly sliced

400g (14oz) carrots, peeled and thinly sliced

800g (1¾lb) sweet potatoes, peeled and cut into 1cm (½in) chunks

1.25 litres (2 pints 4fl oz) hot vegetable stock

Salt and freshly ground black pepper

Double cream, to serve (optional)

1. Heat the butter and oil in a large stockpot or saucepan over a medium heat. When the butter has melted, add the vegetables and fry for 3–4 minutes until starting to soften. Cover and sweat for about 10 minutes, stirring occasionally.

2. Pour in the stock and bring to the boil, then cover with a lid, reduce the heat and simmer for 10 minutes or until the vegetables are tender.

3. Remove from the heat and use a slotted spoon to scoop out half the vegetables into a bowl (see tip). Whizz the remaining soup until smooth, either using a hand blender or in a free-standing blender or food processor. Return the soup to the pan (if blending separately), add the reserved vegetables and season to taste with salt and pepper.

4. Serve hot with a swirl of double cream, if you like, and some crusty bread.

PREPARE AHEAD

Can be made up to 3 days ahead and reheated to serve.

FREEZE *Freezes well (without the cream).*

MARY'S EVERYDAY TIP

You can purée all of the vegetables if you prefer, but I like them partly chunky.

JERUSALEM ARTICHOKE AND CELERY SOUP

With its rich and nutty flavour, this soup is a real treat – best served in small bowls as it's very rich. Jerusalem artichokes are a winter vegetable with knobbly, elongated tubers vaguely resembling root ginger in appearance, and a crisp texture when raw. They vary in colour from pale brown to white, red or purple. Parsnips would make a good alternative if you can't get hold of them or if they are not in season.

SERVES 6

COOK TIME:
50 MINUTES

1 tbsp oil

1 large onion, finely chopped

4 celery sticks, chopped

750g (1lb 10oz) Jerusalem artichokes, scrubbed and cut into 5mm (¼in) slices

1 x 187ml bottle of white wine

1 litre (1¾ pints) vegetable or chicken stock

100ml (3½fl oz) double cream, plus extra to serve

1 tbsp snipped chives, plus extra to garnish

Salt and freshly ground black pepper

1. Heat the oil in a large saucepan and add the onion and celery. Fry over a high heat for a minute, then cover with a lid, reduce the heat to low and cook for about 10 minutes until nearly soft.

2. Add the Jerusalem artichokes and stir over a high heat for 3–4 minutes until they start to brown. Pour in the wine and boil for 2 minutes (see tip) before adding the stock. Bring back up to the boil, then cover with a lid, reduce the heat and simmer for about 25 minutes or until all the vegetables are tender.

3. Season with salt and pepper and then stir in the cream and chives. Blend until smooth, either with a hand blender or in a free-standing blender or food processor.

4. Serve in warmed bowls with a swirl of cream and a few chopped chives.

PREPARE AHEAD

Can be made up to a day ahead and reheated.

FREEZE *Freezes well.*

MARY'S EVERYDAY TIP

It's important to let the wine bubble for 2 minutes before adding the stock, so that the alcohol is cooked out. This process also deglazes the pan, so stir it well to incorporate all the cooked vegetable pieces from the bottom of the pan, for extra flavour.

CELERIAC SOUP WITH CRISPY PANCETTA AND POPPY SEED CROUTONS

Such a warming, healthy and hearty soup, this really is a meal in itself. It has a creamy texture complemented to perfection by the crisp pancetta and croutons and fresh sprigs of watercress.

SERVES 6–8

COOK TIME:
30 MINUTES

FOR THE TOPPING
6 rashers of pancetta, cut into small pieces

FOR THE SOUP
50g (2oz) butter
2 onions, finely chopped
800g (13/4lb) celeriac, peeled and cut into 2cm (¾in) chunks
400g (14oz) potato (2 large), peeled and cut into 2cm (¾in) chunks
1.5 litres (21/2 pints) vegetable or chicken stock
4 tbsp pouring double cream
Salt and freshly ground black pepper

FOR THE CROUTONS
2 medium slices of stale white bread (see tip), crusts removed
2 tbsp oil
1 tbsp poppy seeds
2 tbsp finely grated Parmesan cheese

FOR THE GARNISH
Small watercress leaves, any thick stems removed

1. Preheat the oven to 200°C/180°C fan/Gas 6.

2. Dry-fry the pancetta until crisp in a large saucepan. Transfer with a slotted spoon to a plate, cover with foil and set aside to keep warm.

3. Melt the butter in the pan (no need to clean it first), add the onion, celeriac and potato (see tip) and toss over a high heat for 3–4 minutes or until starting to brown. Pour in the stock, season with salt and pepper and bring to the boil. Leave to bubble for 4–5 minutes, then cover, reduce the heat and simmer for about 15 minutes or until the vegetables are tender.

4. Meanwhile, make the croutons. Cut the bread into batons about 1 x 5cm (½ x 2in) in size. Place in a wide bowl with the oil, poppy seeds and Parmesan and toss until coated, seasoning with salt and pepper. Arrange in a single layer on a baking sheet and cook in the oven for 8–10 minutes, turning halfway through, until golden and crisp.

5. When the vegetables are tender, spoon them and half the liquid into a blender or food processor and whizz until smooth. (Alternatively, transfer to a high-sided jug or bowl and whizz using a hand blender.) Return the vegetable purée to the saucepan, stirring well to combine everything, then pour in the cream and check the seasoning, adding salt and pepper to taste. Heat through until piping hot.

6. Serve the soup in warmed bowls with a scattering of pancetta, watercress and croutons to serve.

PREPARE AHEAD

The soup can be made up to 2 days ahead and reheated.

The croutons can be made up to 2 days ahead and reheated to crisp up before serving.

MARY'S EVERYDAY TIPS

It's best to use stale bread for the croutons, as fresh bread will soak up too much liquid.

Adding the potato stabilises the soup, ensuring that it does not separate.

SMOKED HADDOCK AND ASPARAGUS CHOWDER

This chunky fish soup, full of goodness and rich flavour, makes a hearty meal in itself. A chowder is a creamy, thick soup generally made with fish. There are many variations, the English version traditionally including potato, as I've done here.

SERVES 6

COOK TIME:
25–30 MINUTES

18 fine asparagus spears

25g (1oz) butter

2 small leeks, sliced into thin rounds

2 tbsp plain flour

450ml (15fl oz) hot fish or vegetable stock

600ml (1 pint) full-fat milk

2 small carrots, peeled and cut into small chunks

1 large potato, peeled and cut into small chunks

500g (1lb 2oz) undyed smoked haddock, skin removed (see tip on page 156) and cut into chunks

Salt and freshly ground black pepper

FOR THE GARNISH

1 tbsp snipped chives

1. Cut off the tips of the asparagus spears, about 5cm (2in) long, and finely chop the rest of the spears.

2. Melt the butter in a saucepan, add the leeks and stir over a high heat for 2–3 minutes. Sprinkle in the flour and cook for 30 seconds, stirring. Blend in first the stock and then the milk, stirring until smooth, and bring to the boil.

3. Add the carrots and potato, and season with salt and pepper. Bring back up to the boil, then cover with a lid, reduce the heat to low and simmer for 10–15 minutes, stirring occasionally, until the vegetables are tender.

4. Meanwhile, cook the asparagus (the tips and chopped pieces) in boiling salted water for 2 minutes, drain and refresh in cold water.

5. Add the haddock to the hot soup (see tip) and stir for 3–4 minutes until just cooked. Add the chopped asparagus, saving the tips for garnishing later, and stir.

6. Spoon into warmed bowls, top with the chopped chives and 3 asparagus tips per bowl. Serve with crusty bread.

PREPARE AHEAD

The base of the soup can be made up to a day ahead and then reheated, the fish and asparagus added to serve.

MARY'S EVERYDAY TIP

Adding the fish to the hot sauce gently cooks it. Be careful not to over-stir the mixture, however, to avoid breaking up the chunks of fish.

MUSHROOM BRUSCHETTA

Crisp slices of ciabatta topped with a fragrant herby mixture of chestnut and wild mushrooms – perfect for either a starter or light lunch. Don't throw away the mushroom soaking liquid; it can be used in any recipes that require stock. Add it to soups, gravy, risotto or even bolognese (see page 94).

SERVES 4

COOK TIME: 10 MINUTES, PLUS SOAKING

20g (¾oz) dried wild mushrooms

1 ready-to-bake ciabatta loaf

2 tbsp olive oil

Sea salt flakes, for sprinkling

Leaves from 1 sprig of rosemary, chopped (optional)

50g (2oz) butter

½ white onion, finely chopped

2 garlic cloves, crushed

250g (9oz) chestnut mushrooms, sliced

2 tbsp chopped tarragon, plus whole sprigs to garnish

125g (4½oz) full-fat cream cheese

½ tsp truffle oil

Salt and freshly ground black pepper

1. Cover the dried mushrooms in boiling water and leave to soak for 15 minutes.

2. Cut two slices of ciabatta per person, brush each slice on one side with olive oil and sprinkle with sea salt flakes and chopped rosemary if using. Set aside while you make the topping.

3. Melt the butter in a frying pan and fry the onion and garlic over a medium heat for 2–3 minutes until golden. Add the sliced chestnut mushrooms and cook for 3–4 minutes, stirring occasionally.

4. Drain the wild mushrooms, reserving the juice (see introduction and tip). Add the mushrooms to the pan and cook the mixture until soft and all the liquid has evaporated. Season with salt and pepper, then add the chopped tarragon and the cream cheese and stir well. Remove from the heat and add the truffle oil.

5. Toast the ciabatta on both sides until golden brown in a griddle pan or small dry frying pan. Top with the mushroom mixture and garnish with tarragon sprigs to serve.

MARY'S EVERYDAY TIPS

If some of the wild mushrooms are in very large pieces, you may wish to cut them smaller after they have soaked.

Truffle oil is a very strong flavour, hence only using a little. If you really like it, drizzle a little over to serve.

HERBED BLINIS WITH PEAS AND PANCETTA

This dish is super for a starter or a light lunch – very summery with the mint, basil and peas. If fresh peas are in season, use the same quantity as indicated below. Rashers of pancetta look great kept in a long strip for this rather than chopped. Thinly sliced pancetta can be sticky to handle, however, so keep it in the fridge until it is ready to be cooked. When chilled, the thin sheets should separate more easily.

SERVES 4

COOK TIME:
15–20 MINUTES

FOR THE BLINIS

175g (6oz) self-raising flour

1 tsp baking powder

1 egg, beaten

200–225ml (7–8fl oz) milk

½ tbsp finely chopped
    mint, plus whole leaves
    to garnish

½ tbsp finely chopped basil

1–2 tbsp oil

Salt and freshly ground
    black pepper

FOR THE TOPPING

8 rashers of pancetta or
    streaky bacon

200g (7oz) frozen petits
    pois, defrosted

50g (2oz) feta cheese,
    crumbled

Juice and finely grated
    zest of ½ lemon

1 tbsp olive oil

½ tbsp finely chopped mint

½ tbsp finely chopped basil

1. First make the blinis. Sift the flour, baking powder and a pinch of salt into a bowl. Add the egg, then gradually stir in 200ml (7fl oz) of the milk and gently whisk into a smooth batter. The texture should be dropping consistency – if too thick, add a touch more milk. Mix in the mint and basil.

2. Heat a non-stick frying pan over a high heat and rub some of the oil into the pan. Add a tablespoonful of the herbed batter to the pan, using the spoon to tease the edges of the batter into a neat disc. There is enough batter for eight blinis (see tip), which you will need to make in batches.

3. Cook each batch over a high heat for a couple of minutes until bubbles appear in the surface and the edges start to curl (see tip). Use a fish slice or small palette knife to carefully turn them over and cook on the other side for another 2 minutes or until golden. Remove from the pan and set aside.

4. Next make the topping. Add the pancetta or bacon to the pan and dry-fry until golden and crisp. Set aside.

5. Measure the peas in a bowl and mash with a potato masher until crushed but not puréed. Add the feta, lemon juice and zest with the olive oil and herbs, season with pepper and a little salt and stir together. Add to the hot pan and cook for 30 seconds to heat through.

6. Arrange two blinis on each plate, with a spoonful of pea mix and two rashers of pancetta on top.

PREPARE AHEAD

The blinis can be made up to 4 hours ahead. Refresh in a hot oven for a few minutes before serving.

The pea mix can be prepared up to 6 hours ahead.

FREEZE *Freezes well.*

MARY'S EVERYDAY TIP

When they are cooked on one side, the blinis will lift easily when a palette knife is inserted underneath. If they are still sticking to the pan, they are not ready to be turned and would tear.

TWO-SIDED HERBED SMOKED SALMON AND HORSERADISH PÂTÉ

This is such an impressive-looking dish and it can be prepared well ahead. The creamy pâté is sandwiched between smoked salmon slices and finely chopped herbs in an intense green layer. I love the combination of horseradish and smoked salmon here; it gives the pâté a real boost.

SERVES 8

**PREP TIME:
20 MINUTES, PLUS
CHILLING AND
FREEZING**

300g (11oz) smoked salmon slices (see tip)

75g (3oz) butter, softened

100g (4oz) full-fat crème fraîche

180g (6oz) full-fat cream cheese

Juice of 1 small lemon

3 tbsp hot horseradish sauce from a jar

2 tbsp finely chopped dill

2 tbsp finely chopped flat-leaf parsley

Salt and freshly ground black pepper

TO SERVE

Lamb's lettuce

8 lemon wedges

1. You will need an 18cm (7in) square baking tin. Line the tin with a sheet of cling film that is large enough to come over the sides of the tin.

2. Line the base of the tin with a third of the smoked salmon slices, trimming any uneven edges so the salmon fits well. (Four slices fit neatly with the long edge against the side and the pointed edge of the slice towards the middle.) Cut the remaining slices into large pieces.

3. Measure the butter, crème fraîche and cream cheese into a food processor and whizz until combined. Add the remaining smoked salmon with the lemon juice, horseradish sauce and some black pepper, and whizz again until roughly chopped. Check the seasoning, adding salt if you like, though the salmon is probably salty enough.

4. Spread the mixture over the salmon in the tin, smoothing so the top is level. Scatter the herbs evenly over the top. Lay cling film over the surface and lightly press the herbs into the pâté so the whole top becomes bright green. Chill in the fridge, still covered in cling film, for at least an hour.

5. To serve, leave the pâté in the freezer for about 45 minutes (this makes it easier to cut). Holding the edges of the cling film, carefully lift the pâté out and turn over (so the salmon is on top) on to a board. Remove the cling film and, using a thin-bladed sharp knife, cut into quarters. Cut each square into four triangles, so you have 16 small, even triangles in total.

6. Arrange the lamb's lettuce on individual plates, sit two triangles on each plate with a wedge of lemon. Serve with brown bread or toast.

PREPARE AHEAD

Can be made up to 2 days ahead and kept stored in the fridge.

FREEZE

Freezes well without the herb layer. Defrost and add herbs to serve.

MARY'S EVERYDAY TIP

To save costs, buy 200g (7oz) of the total smoked salmon as trimmings, as this quantity is whizzed in the food processor anyway.

INDIVIDUAL SMOKED SALMON AND PRAWN STARTERS WITH AVOCADO

I prefer to serve a cold first course, prepared on the plates well ahead – it puts my mind at ease knowing there's one less thing to do at the last minute. Buy the finest cold water prawns and smoked salmon you can. You could also serve this on one big sharing platter, if you liked.

SERVES 6

PREP TIME:
10–15 MINUTES

200g (7oz) small cooked peeled prawns

2 ripe avocados, peeled and sliced (see tip)

Juice of ½ lemon

1 x 70g bag of lamb's lettuce

2 ripe tomatoes, deseeded and sliced into thin strips (see tip)

6 smoked salmon slices

1 tbsp snipped chives

6 sprigs of dill

FOR THE COCKTAIL SAUCE

4 tbsp crème fraîche

1 tbsp tomato ketchup

2 tsp hot horseradish sauce from a jar

2 tsp lemon juice

Salt and freshly ground black pepper

FOR THE DRESSING

1 tsp Dijon mustard

2 tbsp white wine vinegar

90ml (3fl oz) good olive oil

1 tsp sugar

1. In a medium bowl, mix together all of the ingredients for the cocktail sauce and season with salt and pepper. Drain the prawns and dry really well on kitchen paper before adding to the bowl and stirring in.

2. Toss the avocado in the lemon juice in a separate bowl.

3. Arrange six plates on the table. Put a few lettuce leaves on one side of each plate and a helping of prawns in cocktail sauce on top of the lettuce. Arrange the avocado and tomato slices next to the prawns. Curl a slice of salmon and place next to the avocado and tomato. Sprinkle the chives on top of the prawns and lay a sprig of dill on top of the salmon.

4. Whisk all of the dressing ingredients together in a bowl or small jug. Drizzle over the tomatoes and avocado before serving.

PREPARE AHEAD

Can be assembled up to 6 hours ahead and kept in the fridge.

The dressing can be made up to 4 days ahead. Store in a jam jar with a lid and shake well to mix before pouring over.

MARY'S EVERYDAY TIPS

Prepare each avocado by first cutting it in half, then removing the stone with the help of a large knife. Use a large dessert or soup spoon to scoop out the two halves intact, sliding it up underneath the skin, so that the avocado can then be sliced into neat pieces.

Use a small, serrated knife for slicing the tomato thinly.

GRIDDLED HALLOUMI WITH BEETROOT CHUTNEY

This would be great for a starter, summer lunch or as part of a buffet. The halloumi can be fried in a frying pan, if you prefer, but the griddle gives that lovely chargrilled effect.

SERVES 4

COOK TIME:
20 MINUTES, PLUS MARINATING

400g (14oz) halloumi, cut into thin slices

1 tbsp olive oil

1 tsp cumin seeds

3 pitta breads, toasted and sliced into strips, to serve

FOR THE BEETROOT CHUTNEY

200g (7oz) ready-cooked beetroot in natural juices

1 tbsp olive oil

½ red onion, finely chopped

1 garlic clove, crushed

½ tsp ground cumin

¼ tsp cumin seeds

1 tsp white wine vinegar

1 tsp caster sugar

Salt and freshly ground black pepper

1. Brush the halloumi with the olive oil and sprinkle with the cumin seeds. Set aside to marinate for about an hour.

2. Meanwhile, make the chutney. Cut the beetroot into tiny, raisin-sized pieces. Heat the oil in a pan, add the onion and garlic and fry over a medium heat for 3–4 minutes, then cover the pan, lower the heat and sweat for about 10 minutes until soft and tender.

3. Sprinkle in the ground cumin and the cumin seeds and stir well, then add the vinegar and sugar and season with salt and pepper. Cook over a high heat for about 3 minutes, add the beetroot and stir in. Tip into a bowl to cool.

4. Heat a griddle pan until hot, and chargrill the halloumi for 2–3 minutes on each side until ridged and golden (see tip). Serve the halloumi with the chutney and toasted pitta slices and heritage baby tomatoes, if liked.

PREPARE AHEAD

Assemble up to 4 hours ahead.

The chutney can be made up to 2 days ahead.

MARY'S EVERYDAY TIP

The halloumi slices may need to be cooked in two batches: try not to overcrowd the pan, as it will be hard to turn them easily.

MUSHROOM AND THYME PÂTÉ

So easy to make in advance, this would be perfect as a starter or for a weekend lunch.
Serve on crackers or with toasted pitta bread strips.

SERVES 4–6

COOK TIME:
6–8 MINUTES, PLUS
COOLING AND
CHILLING

A large knob of butter

1 banana shallot,
 finely chopped

250g (9oz) chestnut
 mushrooms, sliced

1 small garlic clove, crushed

50g (2oz) fresh white
 breadcrumbs

75g (3oz) butter, softened

100g (4oz) full-fat
 cream cheese

1 tbsp chopped parsley

1 tbsp chopped thyme leaves,
 plus sprigs to garnish

1 tbsp lemon juice

1 tsp soy sauce (see tip)

A little freshly grated nutmeg

Salt and freshly ground
 black pepper

1. Melt the butter in a large frying pan, add the shallot and fry over a high heat for 2–3 minutes. Add the mushrooms and garlic and fry for another 4–5 minutes until the liquid has evaporated and the mushrooms are lightly golden. Transfer to a plate to cool down for 5 minutes.

2. Tip the mixture into a food processor and whizz until roughly chopped. Add the remaining ingredients and season with salt and pepper. Scrape down the sides of the processor bowl with a spatula and whizz again until combined but still with a little texture rather than completely smooth.

3. Spoon the pâté into a serving bowl or four ramekins. Chill in the fridge for 2 hours and bring to room temperature to serve, sprinkled with fresh thyme sprigs, if you like.

PREPARE AHEAD

Can be made up to 3 days ahead and kept chilled in the fridge.

MARY'S EVERYDAY TIPS

The soy sauce gives colour and flavour to the pâté.

Any leftover pâté can be used as a sandwich filling the next day.

CRISPY BACON RÖSTI WITH FRIED EGG

Rösti is such a favourite of mine – a layer of crispy potato with fried onion and savoury pieces of smoked bacon. Serve with a fried egg on top for a casual weekend brunch.

SERVES 2

COOK TIME:
50 MINUTES

2–3 tbsp sunflower oil

2 rashers of smoked back bacon, cut into small pieces

1 small onion, thinly sliced

500g (1lb 2oz) floury potatoes, peeled

2 eggs

Salt and freshly ground black pepper

1. You will need a 20cm (8in) omelette pan or non-stick frying pan (see tip).

2. Heat 1 tablespoon of the sunflower oil in the pan, add the bacon pieces and fry over a high heat for 3–4 minutes or until crisp. Remove the bacon using a slotted spoon and set aside. Add the onion to the pan and fry for a minute, then cover with a lid, reduce the heat to low and sweat for 15 minutes until soft and tender.

3. Coarsely grate the peeled raw potatoes, then wrap in a clean tea towel and squeeze to wring out as much water – this prevents the rösti from being soggy (see tip).

4. Tip the grated raw potato into a bowl, add the softened onion and crispy bacon, season with salt and pepper and mix well.

5. Heat the remaining oil in the pan (no need to clean it first), then add the potato mixture, using the back of a spoon to press the mixture into the pan and spread it in an even layer right to the edges.

6. Cook over a low heat for 10–15 minutes, then slide a fish slice under to loosen the base and carefully turn over. The easiest way to do this is to invert the rösti on to a plate before sliding it back into the pan; you may need to add a little more oil first. Cook the other side for 10–15 minutes until both sides are golden and crisp.

7. In separate pan, fry the eggs in a little hot oil for 3–4 minutes, or until done to your liking, and serve one egg per person on top of half the crispy hot rösti.

PREPARE AHEAD

Best made and served straight away, but can be re-fried in the pan.

MARY'S EVERYDAY TIP

It's so important to use a small pan for making rösti. If you use a large pan, it will be tricky to make it crisp. It's equally important to wring out the liquid from the grated potatoes before frying. If either step is not followed, it could result in soggy rösti. Grate the potatoes at the last minute and do not put them in water or the starch will be washed off, and it's the starch that holds the mixture together.

BEEF, PORK,
LAMB AND
GAME

Meat dishes form the backbone of most family meals, and in this chapter I have suggested everyday favourites with simple twists to make them extra special, like my Venison Cottage Pie (page 115).

BEEF AND ALE STEW WITH HORSERADISH SPIRAL DUMPLINGS

Hearty and warming, this is such a great dish to serve a crowd. Virtually a meal in itself, it needs just a green vegetable to go with it. When cut, the dumpling mixture forms lovely spiral shapes in cross-section that make this classic dish just that little bit different.

SERVES 8

COOK TIME:
2½–3 HOURS

FOR THE STEW

2–3 tbsp oil

1kg (2lb 3oz) braising beef, diced (see tip)

250g (9oz) small shallots, peeled and halved

2 carrots, peeled and thinly sliced

200g (7oz) button mushrooms

50g (2oz) plain flour

500ml (18fl oz) ale

150ml (5fl oz) beef stock

2–3 tbsp onion marmalade or caramelised onion chutney

1–2 tbsp Worcestershire sauce

A dash of gravy browning (optional)

3 bay leaves

Salt and freshly ground black pepper

FOR THE DUMPLINGS

175g (6oz) self-raising flour, plus extra for dusting

75g (3oz) shredded suet (beef or vegetable)

3–4 tbsp hot horseradish sauce

2 tbsp chopped parsley

1. You will need a 4-litre (7-pint) deep flameproof and ovenproof casserole dish with a lid. Preheat the oven to 160°C/140°C fan/Gas 3.

2. Heat 2 tablespoons of the oil in the casserole dish, add the beef and brown all over on a high heat – you will need to do this in batches, removing the meat with a slotted spoon as it is cooked and setting aside.

3. Pour in a little more oil if needed and add the shallots with the carrots and mushrooms. Stir-fry over a high heat for 4–5 minutes.

4. Measure the flour into a bowl and gradually whisk in the ale, slowly at first to make a smooth paste before adding the rest of the ale.

5. Return the meat to the casserole dish, then pour in the flour mixture and the stock. Stir over a high heat until the liquid is thickened and bubbling. Add the onion marmalade/chutney, Worcestershire sauce, gravy browning (if using) and bay leaves. Season with salt and pepper, then stir as you bring back up to the boil and allow to bubble for a couple of minutes. Cover with the lid and transfer to the oven to cook for 2–2½ hours or until the meat is tender.

6. To make the dumplings, measure the flour and suet into a bowl and season with salt and pepper. Gradually stir in 125–150ml (4–5fl oz) of water to make a soft, sticky dough (see tip). Transfer to a floured work surface and gently knead until smooth.

7. Sprinkle flour on to a sheet of baking paper, sit the dough on top and roll into a rectangle about 15 x 25cm (6 x 10in). Spread the top with the horseradish sauce and scatter with the parsley. Roll up the dough into a Swiss roll, working from the long side and using the baking paper to help. Chill in the fridge for 45 minutes and slice into eight using a serrated knife (see tip).

Recipe continues overleaf

8. When the meat is tender, remove from the oven and increase the temperature to 220°C/200°C fan/Gas 7. Remove the lid from the casserole and arrange the dumplings, spiral side up and spaced apart, on top of the stew. Return to the oven and cook, uncovered, for about 25 minutes or until the dumplings are golden and puffed up.

9. Remove the bay leaves and serve piping hot with buttered cabbage.

PREPARE AHEAD

The stew can be made up to a day ahead and reheated with the freshly made dumplings on top. Bring to the boil on the hob before putting into the hot oven.

FREEZE

Freezes well without the dumplings.

The raw dumpling roulade can be frozen. Defrost, then slice as in step 7 and place on top when reheating the stew.

MARY'S EVERYDAY TIPS

Cut up the beef into pieces that are all the same size so they cook at the same rate.

A wetter dough is better as it will be less tough when cooked.

A serrated knife will help when slicing the dumplings to prevent squashing the dough and losing the spiral effect.

CHILLI CON CARNE

This is a great everyday supper dish for the family. The long slow cooking makes all the difference, so don't try and rush it! The meat softens in the oven and the flavours combine together properly.

SERVES 6

COOK TIME: 1 HOUR 40 MINUTES

2 tbsp olive oil

3 banana shallots, finely chopped

3 garlic cloves, crushed

2 fresh red chillies, deseeded and finely chopped

900g (2lb) minced beef

1 tbsp sweet smoked paprika

1 tbsp ground coriander

½ tsp chilli powder

2 tbsp tomato purée

2 x 400g tins of chopped tomatoes

150ml (5fl oz) beef stock or water

1 x 400g tin of kidney beans, drained and rinsed (see tip)

1 tsp sugar

Salt and freshly ground black pepper

1. Heat the oil in a large deep pan, add the shallots, garlic and chillies and fry over a high heat for 4–5 minutes. Add the mince and toss in the pan until browned all over.

2. Sprinkle in the spices and fry for a further minute, then add the tomato purée, tinned tomatoes, stock or water, kidney beans and sugar. Give everything a good stir and season with salt and pepper.

3. Bring to the boil, then reduce the heat, cover with a lid and simmer for about 1½ hours or until tender. Make sure the pan is properly covered as it simmers or it will dry out. If your pan doesn't have a lid, cover it with a sheet of foil and scrunch it down well around the edges to seal in the steam.

4. Serve hot with rice or in taco shells with grated Cheddar and a dollop of soured cream on top (see also tip).

PREPARE AHEAD

Can be made up to a day ahead and reheated.

FREEZE *The cooked dish freezes well.*

MARY'S EVERYDAY TIPS

Drain the kidney beans and rinse them well under running water to remove all the liquid they have been canned in.

If this dish is too hot for anyone, serve their portion with a spoonful of soured cream or crème fraîche/Greek yoghurt on top. Once stirred in, this will tone down the effect of the chilli, while the rest of the diners can enjoy the heat.

FILLET STEAK WITH PEPPERCORN SAUCE

Pan-fried steaks always make such a quick and tasty meal, made extra special here with the luxurious peppercorn sauce. Perfect for a relaxed supper with friends, enjoyed with a nice glass of red wine.

SERVES 4

COOK TIME:
10 MINUTES

4 x 150g (5oz) centre-cut
   fillet steaks (see tip)

50g (2oz) butter

100ml (3½fl oz) beef stock

½ garlic clove, crushed

2 tbsp brandy

1 tbsp Worcestershire sauce

1 tbsp Dijon mustard

150ml (5fl oz) pouring
   double cream

½ tsp crushed black
   peppercorns (see tip)

2 tbsp chopped parsley,
   plus extra to garnish

Salt and freshly ground
   black pepper

1. Place the steaks between two pieces of cling film and flatten with your hand to about 5mm (⅛in) thick. Spread the butter over the steaks on both sides and season well with salt and pepper.

2. Heat a large non-stick frying pan or griddle pan until hot, add the steaks and fry over a high heat for 2 minutes on each side (see tip). Lift out to rest and keep warm, loosely covered in foil.

3. Pour the stock into the pan (no need to clean it first) and boil to reduce by half, then add the garlic, brandy, Worcestershire sauce, mustard, cream and crushed black peppercorns. Stir together as you bring to the boil over a high heat. Season with salt and allow the sauce to bubble away for a couple of minutes to reduce slightly – the consistency should be the thickness of pouring cream. Stir in the parsley and remove from the heat.

4. Spoon the sauce over the steaks, sprinkle with a little more parsley and serve with sauté potatoes and a green vegetable.

PREPARE AHEAD

The steaks can be fried ahead and, once cooled, kept covered in the fridge for up to 12 hours. Top with a knob of butter and reheat on a baking sheet in a hot oven for 6 minutes. Serve at once.

The sauce can be made up to a day ahead and reheated.

MARY'S EVERYDAY TIPS

Rib-eye steak would also work well for this recipe.

Keep your peppercorns chunky if you like some texture to the sauce.

Cook for 3–4 minutes per side (depending on thickness) for steaks that are more well done.

FILLET BEEF SALAD WITH ASIAN DRESSING

This is such a quick and easy salad to make and it tastes delicious too. The beef is nicely seared but still pink in the middle, while the lentil sprouts add crunch, and the soy and ginger in the dressing give an Asian twist. The steak can be served hot or cold, but carve it just before serving to ensure it stays pink.

SERVES 4–6

COOK TIME:
6 MINUTES, PLUS RESTING

1 tbsp olive oil

2 large fillet steaks (about 200g/7oz each) (see tip)

100g (4oz) rocket

30g (1oz) lentil sprout mix (see tip)

Salt and freshly ground black pepper

FOR THE ASIAN DRESSING

Juice of 1 lime

1 tbsp white wine vinegar

5 tbsp good olive oil

1 tbsp sweet chilli sauce

2 tsp soy sauce

1 tsp grated fresh root ginger (see tip on page 61)

1 tsp muscovado sugar

1. Heat a non-stick frying pan until very hot. Rub the oil into the steaks on each side and season with salt and pepper. Pan-fry the steaks on each side for about 3 minutes, depending on their thickness and how rare you like it – I like to serve it rare. Remove from the pan and set aside to rest for 5 minutes, loosely covered in foil.

2. To make the dressing, measure all the ingredients into a bowl or small jug and whisk to combine.

3. Scatter the rocket leaves over a serving platter and sprinkle over the sprout mix. Thinly slice the steak and arrange on top. Spoon half the dressing over the beef and serve the rest on the side. Serve while the beef is still warm or allow it to cool first.

PREPARE AHEAD

The dressing can be made up to 3 days ahead. Make in a screw-top jar with a lid and keep in the fridge.

MARY'S EVERYDAY TIPS

Instead of using two fillet steaks, if you buy from a butcher you can sometimes get the tail end of the fillet. Two should weigh about 200g and is more reasonable.

Lentil sprout mix can be found in the salad section of a supermarket, but you could use any sprouted beans or seeds and increase the quantity, if you wish. Other sources include farm and health-food shops, or you could sprout your own!

RAGÙ BOLOGNESE WITH PAPPARDELLE

Ragù bolognese is such a classic everyday dish, loved by young and old alike. The traditional Italian version uses minced pork as well as beef, as I've done here. It also has a long, slow cooking time that gives meltingly tender meat and a rich, deep-flavoured sauce, but with a relatively small amount of liquid. If you prefer a runnier sauce, simply add a touch more stock.

SERVES 8

COOK TIME: 2¼ HOURS

450g (1lb) pappardelle or tagliatelle

Parmesan cheese, grated, to serve

Basil leaves, to garnish

FOR THE RAGÙ

2 tbsp olive oil

2 onions, chopped

1 large carrot, peeled and finely diced

2 celery sticks, finely diced

500g (1lb 2oz) lean minced pork

500g (1lb 2oz) lean minced beef

3 garlic cloves, crushed

3 tbsp sun-dried tomato paste

150ml (5fl oz) white wine

500ml (18fl oz) passata

1 x 400g tin of chopped tomatoes

200ml (7fl oz) beef stock

3 bay leaves

2 tbsp chopped thyme leaves

4 tbsp double cream (optional)

Salt and freshly ground black pepper

1. You will need a 3-litre (5-pint) deep flameproof and ovenproof pan or casserole dish, with a lid. Preheat the oven to 160°C/140°C fan/Gas 3.

2. First make the ragù. Heat the oil in the pan, add the onions, carrot and celery and fry over a high heat for 5–6 minutes until the vegetables are starting to soften. Add the minced pork and beef and fry with the vegetables, stirring to break down and seal the meat.

3. When the mince has browned, and any excess liquid has evaporated, add the garlic and fry for 30 seconds. Stir in the sun-dried tomato paste, then pour in the wine and bring to the boil. Add the passata, tinned tomatoes, stock and herbs. Season with salt and pepper and bring back up to the boil, then cover with a lid and transfer to the oven to cook for about an hour (see tip).

4. After an hour, remove the lid from the pan and stir in the cream if using, then put back in the oven to cook, uncovered, for another hour until tender and reduced. Remove the bay leaves before serving.

5. Shortly before the ragù has finished cooking, cook the pasta in boiling salted water in a large pan according to the packet instructions. Drain and divide between plates, then spoon over the ragù and serve scattered with freshly grated Parmesan and garnished with a few basil leaves.

PREPARE AHEAD

The ragù can be made up to a day ahead and reheated.

FREEZE *The cooked ragù freezes well.*

MARY'S EVERYDAY TIP

Cooking in the oven provides an even, all-round source of heat and gives the ragù a real depth of flavour, but you can cook on a low heat on the hob, if you prefer, for the same length of time.

MARY'S SAUSAGES

A bit like a cross between toad in the hole and macaroni cheese, this dish will be a real winner with the family! It's also perfect for using up any leftover cooked carrots and leeks. I've included Cumberland sausages, but you can substitute with your favourite type.

SERVES 6

**COOK TIME:
55 MINUTES**

12 Cumberland sausages

3 large carrots, peeled and diced into 1cm (½in) pieces

3 leeks, thickly sliced

3 large potatoes, peeled and cut into 2cm (¾in) chunks

FOR THE SAUCE

50g (2oz) butter

50g (2oz) plain flour

750ml (1 pint 6fl oz) vegetable or chicken stock

3 tbsp double cream

2 tbsp snipped chives, plus extra to serve

25g (1oz) Cheddar cheese, grated

Salt and freshly ground black pepper

1. You will need a 2-litre (3½-pint) wide-based, deep ovenproof dish. Preheat the oven to 200°C/180°C fan/Gas 6.

2. Arrange the sausages in a roasting tin and roast in the oven for 20–25 minutes until golden brown on one side.

3. Meanwhile, put the carrots and leeks into a large saucepan and cover with water, then bring to the boil and boil for 5 minutes. Add the potatoes and boil for a further 6 minutes or until the potatoes are tender. Drain and set aside.

4. To make the sauce, melt the butter in another saucepan over a gentle heat, add the flour and whisk until combined into a smooth paste (see tip). With the pan still over the heat, gradually add the stock a bit at a time, whisking well until smooth. Then increase the heat until the sauce is thickened and bubbling. Add the cream and chives and season with salt and pepper.

5. Tip the cooked vegetables into the ovenproof dish and pour over the sauce. Sprinkle over the cheese. Arrange the sausages, browned side down, in the dish. Cook for 20–25 minutes until golden and bubbling. Serve piping hot.

PREPARE AHEAD

Can be cooked and assembled in the dish up to 6 hours ahead.

MARY'S EVERYDAY TIP

Using a whisk gives a smooth white sauce.

HOMEMADE PIZZA WITH PARMA HAM AND GOAT'S CHEESE

There can be nothing nicer than a homemade pizza, and this one is particularly straightforward to make, as the dough for the base only needs to rise once. The caramelised onions add a lovely sweetness to the topping. They are easy to prepare, but if time is short, you could always use caramelised onions from a jar. You'll need soft goat's cheese for this recipe – the type that comes in a tub and can be dolloped easily over the top of the pizza.

SERVES 4–6

COOK TIME:
35–40 MINUTES,
PLUS RISING

FOR THE DOUGH

250g (9oz) strong white flour, plus extra for dusting

1 tsp fast-action dried yeast (see tip)

1 tbsp olive oil, plus extra for greasing and drizzling

1 small garlic clove, crushed

½ tsp salt

150–175ml (5–6fl oz) lukewarm water

FOR THE TOPPING

1 tbsp olive oil

2 onions, thinly sliced

1 tbsp light muscovado sugar

1 tbsp balsamic vinegar

150ml (5fl oz) passata

8 slices of Parma ham

200g (7oz) soft goat's cheese

Salt and freshly ground black pepper

Basil leaves, to garnish

1. To make the dough, measure the flour, yeast and olive oil into a bowl. Add the garlic and salt (on a separate side of the bowl to the yeast – see tip on page 49), then gradually pour in the warm water (you may not need it all) and stir with a wooden spoon until combined and a soft dough is formed.

2. Tip on to a floured work surface and knead for 10 minutes into a smooth dough. Oil a large clean bowl, sit the dough in the bowl and cover with cling film. Place in a warm place and leave to rise for 1–1½ hours or until doubled in size. If making in a food mixer fitted with a dough hook, this will take about 4 minutes.

3. Meanwhile, caramelise the onions for the topping. Heat the oil in a frying pan, add the onions and fry over a medium heat for 4–5 minutes until beginning to soften. Cover with a lid and sweat over a low heat for about 15 minutes until soft. Remove the lid, add the sugar and balsamic vinegar, then turn up the heat and stir-fry for 3–4 minutes until golden brown and sticky. Set aside to cool.

4. Preheat the oven to 240°C/220°C fan/Gas 9 and place a large baking sheet inside to get very hot.

5. Once the dough has doubled in size, tip on to a floured work surface and knead into a round to lightly knock it back. Use your fingers or knuckles to push the dough out into a circle about 30cm (12in) in diameter, slightly thicker at the edges to form the crust of the pizza. Place on a sheet of baking paper spread over a flat baking sheet.

Recipe continues overleaf

6. Season the passata with salt and pepper and spread on top of the dough. Scatter with the caramelised onions, then scrunch up the Parma-ham slices and arrange on top before adding dollops of the goat's cheese. Slide the baking paper with the assembled pizza on top on to the hot baking sheet and bake for 12–15 minutes or until golden on top and the dough is cooked.

7. Garnish with basil leaves, drizzle with olive oil and serve with dressed salad leaves.

PREPARE AHEAD

The dough can be made with a cold rise in the fridge up to 8 hours ahead; cover very loosely with cling film as it will more than double in size.

The onions can be caramelised up to 2 days ahead.

FREEZE

The risen dough can be frozen up to a month ahead. Make double and freeze half, defrosting before shaping into a circle and adding the topping.

MARY'S EVERYDAY TIP

Instant yeast is a dried rather than fresh form of yeast, giving a quicker rise as it does not need to ferment. It comes in a packet (labelled 'easy blend' or 'quick' yeast) and will last for a long time in your store cupboard.

SAUSAGE AND HERB PLAIT

This is great to make and serve for a family supper during the week, or for a special gathering. Shop-bought puff pastry is excellent; buy the all-butter kind as it tastes as good as homemade. And buy the best sausage meat you can, or take six fat sausages, remove the skin and use the meat for the filling.

SERVES 6–8

COOK TIME:
35–40 MINUTES

½ onion, finely chopped

450g (1lb) pork sausage meat

Finely grated zest of ½ lemon

50g (2oz) sun-blushed
   tomatoes (see tip),
   finely chopped

2 tbsp chopped parsley

1 tbsp chopped thyme leaves

1 x 375g packet of
   ready-rolled, all-butter
   puff pastry

Plain flour, for dusting

1 egg, beaten

Salt and freshly ground
   black pepper

1. Preheat the oven to 220°C/200°C fan/Gas 7. Place a large baking sheet in the oven to get hot.

2. For the filling, tip the onion into a small saucepan, cover with water and boil for about 5 minutes or until tender. Drain and set aside to cool.

3. Measure the sausage meat into a bowl, add the lemon zest, chopped tomatoes and herbs, season with salt and pepper and mix with your hands to combine. Add the cooled onion and mix again.

4. Roll out the pastry on a lightly floured work surface into a rectangle roughly 20 x 40cm (8 x 16in) in size and about the thickness of a £1 coin. Transfer to a sheet of baking paper.

5. Arrange the sausage meat lengthways in the middle of the pastry, leaving a margin of about a third of the pastry on either side and about 5cm (2in) at each end. Brush all over with some of the beaten egg. Fold up the two ends of the pastry over the sausage meat. Leaving a gap of about 1cm (½in) from the sausage meat, cut the pastry on either side into long strips about 2cm (¾in) wide. Fold each strip on top of the sausage meat, alternating from side to side to create a plait.

6. Brush the top of the pastry and the ends with more beaten egg and carefully slide the non-stick paper, with the sausage plait on top, on to the hot baking sheet.

7. Bake for about 35 minutes or until golden all over and brown and crisp on the bottom. Serve hot with dressed salad leaves.

PREPARE AHEAD

Can be made up to 6 hours ahead and cooked to serve or reheated the following day.

FREEZE *Freezes well, cooked or uncooked.*

MARY'S EVERYDAY TIP

If you can't get sun-blushed tomatoes, you can use sun-dried instead, but sun-blushed are more moist and fleshy.

GLAZED HAM WITH FRESH PICCALILLI

Boiling the ham first and then finishing it in the oven makes for a wonderfully tender joint that slices well without crumbling. Once cooked, ham makes a great everyday standby to have in the fridge. I like to cook a small joint (not like the great big ones I serve at Christmas!) and have it for lunch during the week. The piccalilli is lovely, with the right balance of sweet and sharp and just enough crunch. It's darker in colour than the kind you buy in a jar, and, being fresh, is ready to eat straight away.

SERVES 4–6

COOK TIME: 1 HOUR
20–30 MINUTES, PLUS
COOLING

1.25kg (2lb 12oz) gammon
joint (smoked or unsmoked,
according to preference)

10 black peppercorns

3 bay leaves

1 tbsp Dijon mustard

1 tbsp light muscovado sugar

FOR THE PICCALILLI

150ml (5fl oz) malt vinegar

1 tbsp yellow mustard seeds

200g (7oz) cauliflower, cut
into 2cm florets

1 shallot, finely chopped

4 pickled silverskin onions
from a jar, quartered if large

1 garlic clove, crushed

½ small carrot, peeled and
cut into 5mm (¼in) dice

1 tbsp mustard powder

½ tbsp ground turmeric

1 tsp ground ginger

1 tbsp plain flour

50ml (2fl oz) white
wine vinegar

75g (3oz) light
muscovado sugar

Salt and freshly ground
black pepper

1. First cook the gammon. Place in a large saucepan, cover with water, add the peppercorns and bay leaves and bring to the boil. Boil for a couple of minutes, skimming away any scum that rises to the surface, then lower the heat to a simmer, cover with a lid and cook gently for about 1 hour or until cooked through. Remove the gammon from the cooking liquid and set aside to cool on a baking tray.

2. Preheat the oven to 220°C/200°C fan/Gas 7.

3. Wrap foil around the flesh of the cold ham, leaving the fat exposed, so that it does not dry out. Remove any skin and score the fat. Mix the mustard and sugar together in a bowl and spread over the scored fat. Cook in the oven for 20–30 minutes or until the fat is golden brown and bubbling.

4. Meanwhile, make the piccalilli. Measure the malt vinegar and mustard seeds into a large saucepan, then add 75ml (2½fl oz) of water and bring to the boil. Once the water is boiling, add the cauliflower, shallot, pearl onions, garlic and chopped carrot, cover with a lid and simmer for about 5 minutes or until starting to become tender. Take off the hob and set aside with the lid on for a further 5 minutes to continue cooking in the residual heat.

5. Measure the mustard powder, turmeric and ginger into a bowl with the flour and white wine vinegar and mix into a smooth paste.

6. Add the sugar to the pan and stir in the mustard mixture. Season with salt and pepper and simmer, uncovered, for a further 10 minutes, until all the vegetables are tender but with a slight bite to them. Set aside to cool.

7. Carve the ham into slices and serve with the piccalilli (see tip).

PREPARE AHEAD

The ham can be roasted 2–3 days ahead.

The piccalilli can be made up to 5 days ahead, the taste becoming stronger with age. The flavours will have developed and matured after 4 days while remaining well balanced. Keep in a covered bowl or jar in the fridge.

MARY'S EVERYDAY TIP

Do not carve the ham until serving as it will turn grey.

PORTUGUESE PORK AND RICE

Tender pork fillet and rice cooked with smoked paprika and tomatoes – great for feeding the family or for a summer lunch with a dressed salad on the side. Romano peppers are the long thin kind. Tender and sweet, they are my favourite type of peppers at the moment. Smoked paprika is very different from the regular variety – the smokiness gives a lovely deep flavour that is perfect for this dish.

SERVES 4–6

COOK TIME:
30 MINUTES

2 tbsp olive oil

450g (1lb) pork fillet, cut into finger-sized strips

2 tsp runny honey

2 shallots, thinly sliced

3 red Romano peppers, deseeded and cut into 3cm (1¼in) chunks

2 garlic cloves, crushed

1 heaped tsp sweet smoked paprika

300g (11oz) long-grain easy-cook rice

1 x 400g tin of chopped tomatoes

325–350ml (11–12fl oz) chicken stock

50g (2oz) pitted black olives, halved

2 tbsp chopped parsley

Salt and freshly ground black pepper

1. Heat 1 tablespoon of the olive oil in a large, non-stick frying pan, add the pork and honey and sear the meat on a high heat until golden all over (see tip). Using a slotted spoon, remove the pork and set aside.

2. Pour the remaining oil into the pan. Add the shallots and peppers and fry over a high heat for 2–3 minutes. Add the garlic and paprika and fry for another minute. Add the rice, tomatoes and 325ml (11fl oz) of the stock. Stir until combined and season with salt and pepper.

3. Bring to the boil, then lower the heat, cover with a lid and simmer for 20 minutes until the rice is cooked. Check the rice mixture halfway through cooking, adding a little more stock if needed. Add the cooked pork and any meat juices and keep on the heat until the pork is hot.

4. Check for seasoning, then stir in the olives and parsley to serve.

PREPARE AHEAD

The pork can be pan-fried ahead.

MARY'S EVERYDAY TIP

When searing the pork, watch out for lots of juices in the pan, which will make the meat 'stew' and not brown. If this happens, remove half the pork with a slotted spoon and brown it in batches, so as not to overcrowd the pan.

RACK OF LAMB WITH SALSA VERDE

A quick and easy roast with lovely tender meat. Try to buy the rack with bones that have been trimmed quite short, as these will sit more delicately on the plate. Made with lots of fresh herbs, and piquant from the anchovies and pickled cucumbers, the salsa verde has a wonderfully intense flavour that offsets the lamb to perfection.

SERVES 6–8

COOK TIME:
25 MINUTES, PLUS
MARINATING AND
RESTING

2 x French-trimmed racks of
lamb (6–8 chops per rack),
chine bone removed
(see tip)

1 garlic clove, crushed

Finely grated zest of 1 lemon

2 tsp runny honey

2 tbsp olive oil

FOR THE SALSA VERDE

Juice of 1 lemon

1 garlic clove, crushed

1 small bunch of flat-leaf
parsley, chopped

1 small bunch of
basil, chopped

8 tinned anchovies,
finely chopped

75g (3oz) dill-pickled
cucumbers (see tip),
finely chopped

1 tsp runny honey

150ml (5fl oz) olive oil

Salt and freshly ground
black pepper

1. Preheat the oven to 220°C/200°C fan/Gas 7.

2. Trim any excess skin from the racks of lamb and score the fat using a sharp knife. Place the garlic, lemon zest, honey and oil in a large, wide-based ovenproof dish and combine. Add the lamb racks and rub all over with the marinade. Cover and leave to marinate for a minimum of 30 minutes.

3. Heat up a large frying pan, place the racks of lamb fat side down into the pan and brown for about 5 minutes or until dark golden brown. Return to the ovenproof dish, browned side up and with the bones facing the middle.

4. Roast in the oven for 18–20 minutes, then remove, cover the dish with foil and leave to rest for 15 minutes.

5. While the lamb is resting, make the salsa verde. Mix all the ingredients together in a bowl and season with a little salt and pepper. Gently warm the salsa in a small pan to serve.

6. Carve the lamb, cutting between the chops, and serve two chops per person with the warmed salsa on the side and some sautéed new potatoes.

PREPARE AHEAD

The lamb can be marinated up to a day ahead.

The salsa can be made up to 3 days ahead, the flavour intensifying the longer it is kept.

FREEZE *The marinated raw lamb freezes well.*

MARY'S EVERYDAY TIPS

Ask your butcher, or an assistant at the meat counter of your local supermarket, to trim the lamb for you.

Dill-pickled cucumbers come in a jar; they are similar to gherkins but sweeter and with finer skin. If you are unable to buy them, use the same quantity of gherkins instead.

HERB-CRUSTED LAMB CUTLETS WITH CREAMY MINT SAUCE

These are ideal for a weekday supper dish. Putting the cutlets in the oven makes cooking them very straightforward once they have been coated. The panko breadcrumbs give a crisp and golden crust while the meat stays moist inside, complemented by the sweet, mint-flavoured sauce.

SERVES 6

COOK TIME:
12–15 MINUTES

12 lamb cutlets, trimmed (see tip)

2 tbsp finely chopped flat-leaf parsley

2 tbsp finely chopped mint

2 tbsp finely chopped sage

2 tbsp finely chopped rosemary leaves

100g (4oz) panko breadcrumbs (see tip)

2 eggs

4 tbsp plain flour

1 tbsp oil

Salt and freshly ground black pepper

FOR THE SAUCE

3 tbsp mint jelly

2 tbsp mint sauce

450ml (15fl oz) double cream

1. Preheat the oven to 220°C/200°C fan/Gas 7.

2. Remove any fat from the outside of the cutlets. Put all the chopped herbs in a bowl, add the breadcrumbs, season with salt and pepper and mix well.

3. Beat the eggs in a shallow bowl and sprinkle the flour into another shallow bowl. Dip each cutlet first in the flour and then the egg, then roll in the herby breadcrumb mixture until coated all over.

4. Heat the oil in a large ovenproof frying pan and pan-fry the cutlets for 1–2 minutes on each side until golden. Arrange the cutlets in a single layer on a non-stick baking tray, sprinkle over any stray breadcrumbs that remain in the bowl, and bake in the oven for 10–12 minutes until golden brown all over.

5. To make the sauce, measure the mint jelly into a saucepan and melt over a low heat, stirring as it melts. Add the mint sauce and then the cream. Heat gently until well combined and the sauce has just warmed through – do not boil. Season with salt and pepper and remove from the heat.

6. Serve the cutlets with the creamy mint sauce and mixed green beans.

PREPARE AHEAD

The cutlets can be coated in the herb crust up to a day ahead. Cover and store in the fridge, then remove 10–15 minutes before cooking to allow to return to room temperature.

The sauce can be made up to 2 days ahead and kept in the fridge. Reheat gently before serving.

FREEZE *The lamb cutlets freeze well uncooked.*

MARY'S EVERYDAY TIPS

Ask your butcher to trim the cutlets for you.

Panko breadcrumbs are my favourite as they stay crisp during cooking and give a lovely texture. But you can use standard dried breadcrumbs instead.

ROAST LEG OF LAMB WITH A GARLIC AND THYME RUB

A roast leg of lamb, carved into slices and served with a rich dark gravy, gives a real sense of occasion, one that evokes memories for the family for years to come. It's perfect for lunch on Sunday, with enough leftovers to enjoy during the week, whether eaten cold with salad or chopped up in a classic shepherd's pie.

SERVES 6

COOK TIME: 1 HOUR 40 MINUTES, PLUS RESTING

5 sprigs of rosemary

2.3kg (5lb 1oz) leg of lamb

FOR THE RUB

3 garlic cloves, crushed

3 tbsp olive oil

2 tbsp chopped thyme leaves

2 tsp sea salt

FOR THE GRAVY

2 heaped tbsp plain flour

200ml (7fl oz) red wine

300ml (10fl oz) beef or lamb stock

1 tbsp redcurrant jelly

A dash of Worcestershire sauce

1. Preheat the oven to 200°C/180°C fan/Gas 6.

2. Lay the rosemary in a roasting tin and sit the leg of lamb on top.

3. Measure the ingredients for the rub into a small bowl or mortar and mash together with a rolling pin or using a pestle. With clean hands, rub this paste all over the top of the lamb.

4. Roast in the oven for 1½ hours or until golden all over but pink in the middle (see tip). Remove from the tin and transfer to a carving board or tray, then cover and leave to rest for 15 minutes.

5. To make the gravy, skim most of the fat from the juices in the roasting tin, leaving 2 tablespoons of fat in the tin. Discard the remaining fat (or save to use another day) and remove the rosemary sprigs.

6. Heat the tin on the hob, sprinkle in the flour and whisk into the hot fat, then add the wine and stock, redcurrant jelly and Worcestershire sauce. Whisk over a high heat, scraping the base of the tin to incorporate all the caramelised juices, until the gravy comes to the boil and has thickened slightly. Boil for about 5 minutes to reduce the liquid slightly, then strain into a warmed sauce boat or jug.

7. Carve the lamb in thin slices and serve with the gravy.

PREPARE AHEAD

The lamb can be covered in the rub up to a day in advance.

The gravy can be made ahead in a saucepan, poured into the roasting tin to incorporate the flavour and then strained, as below.

FREEZE

Any leftover lamb and gravy can be frozen. Place slices of lamb in a freezer-proof container and pour over the gravy to cover, then defrost and reheat for an instant dinner.

MARY'S EVERYDAY TIP

The suggested roasting time results in pork that is pink inside, but increase the cooking time if you prefer meat that is more well done.

LAMB FRICASSEE WITH PEARL BARLEY

Pearl barley is barley with all the bran removed, giving the round, shiny grains a pearlescent white colour. It can be used in soups and stews as a thickener, or to add texture rather than flavour. I have added it to this classic lamb recipe to give it a twist and make it into an all-in-one dish that can be eaten as it is or with just a green vegetable. The fresh herbs offset the rich and creamy stew, helping to lift the colour and flavour to another level.

SERVES 6

COOK TIME:
1¾ HOURS

2 tbsp sunflower oil

1kg (2lb 3oz) lamb
  neck fillet, cut into
  2cm (¾in) dice

500g (1lb 2oz) shallots
  (see tip), halved

3 celery sticks, sliced

3 garlic cloves, crushed

200ml (7fl oz) white wine

250ml (9fl oz) chicken stock

75g (3oz) pearl barley

200g (7oz) button
  mushrooms, sliced

Juice of ½ lemon

3 tbsp chopped mint

4 tbsp chopped
  flat-leaf parsley

200g (7oz) full-fat
  crème fraîche

Salt and freshly ground
  black pepper

1. You will need a 4-litre (7-pint) ovenproof frying pan or flameproof casserole dish, with a lid. Preheat the oven to 160°C/140°C fan/Gas 3.

2. Add the oil to the frying pan or casserole dish and heat until hot. Season the lamb with salt and pepper and fry over a high heat until golden brown all over – you may need to do this in batches (see tip). Remove with a slotted spoon and set aside.

3. Add the shallots, celery and garlic to the pan and fry for a minute. Pour in the wine and stock and bring to the boil. Return the lamb to the pan and add the pearl barley. Bring back up to the boil, season with salt and pepper and then lower the heat, cover with the lid and transfer to the oven to cook for about 1½ hours or until the lamb is tender and the pearl barley is soft.

4. Remove from the oven and stir in the mushrooms, lemon juice, mint, half the parsley and the crème fraîche. Check the seasoning, adding more salt and pepper if needed, and simmer for 4–5 minutes to cook the mushrooms. Spoon into warmed bowls and sprinkle with chopped parsley to serve.

PREPARE AHEAD

Can be made up to a day ahead and reheated, but omitting the barley as it will absorb all the liquid if left overnight. If reheating, cook the barley separately and stir into the fricassee. Alternatively, add the uncooked barley to the casserole and reheat in the oven or on the hob until the barley is cooked, 25–30 minutes, before finishing off the dish as in step 4.

FREEZE *Freezes well without the pearl barley.*

MARY'S EVERYDAY TIPS

Peel the shallots by plunging into boiling water for a couple of minutes. This makes the skins easier to remove when peeling a large number of them.

Frying the lamb in batches helps to give a good colour and to seal in the flavour. Otherwise, the meat starts to stew in its own juices, rather than frying properly.

VENISON COTTAGE PIE

Such an everyday classic, but I have used venison for a change. Minced venison is easy to buy, and gives a richer colour and flavour to the meat sauce, but you could use minced beef instead or half beef and half venison. Maris Piper, King Edward or Desirée potatoes are all perfect for mashing.

SERVES 6–8

COOK TIME: 2 HOURS, PLUS COOLING

2 tbsp oil

6 rashers of smoked streaky bacon, chopped

1 large onion, finely chopped

1 large carrot, finely chopped

Leaves from 2 sprigs of rosemary, chopped

600g (1lb 5oz) minced venison

1 heaped tbsp plain flour

300ml (10fl oz) red wine

500ml (18fl oz) beef or game stock

Salt and freshly ground black pepper

FOR THE MASH

1kg (2lb 3oz) floury potatoes, peeled and cut into 2cm chunks

A knob of butter

A splash of milk

1. You will need a 1.5-litre (2.5-pint) wide-based ovenproof dish, greased.

2. Heat the oil in a large, deep flameproof casserole dish or saucepan. Add the bacon and fry over a high heat for 3–4 minutes or until crisp. Remove with a slotted spoon and set aside. Tip in the onion, carrot and rosemary and fry for 4–5 minutes. Add the mince and stir over the heat for 3–4 minutes or until golden brown, using two spoons to break up into smaller pieces.

3. Sprinkle in the flour and cook for a minute, stirring. Gradually stir in the wine and then boil for a few minutes to reduce by half. Pour in the stock and bring back up to the boil. Return the bacon to the pan, season with salt and pepper and allow to bubble, stirring, for 5–10 minutes. Cover with a lid, reduce the heat and simmer for about 40 minutes or until tender.

4. Spoon the mince into the ovenproof dish and set aside to cool down completely (see tip).

5. Preheat the oven to 200°C/180°C fan/Gas 6 and make the topping.

6. Cook the potatoes in a pan of boiling salted water for about 15 minutes until tender. Drain, add the butter and milk, season with salt and pepper and mash until smooth (see tip).

7. Spoon the mash on top of the cold mince, level the top and rough the surface with the back of a fork, making a pattern, if you like. Bake in the oven for about 45 minutes or until golden and bubbling.

PREPARE AHEAD

Can be prepared and assembled up to a day ahead, ready to cook.

The mince can be made 1–2 days ahead and stored in the fridge.

FREEZE

The cooked mince can be frozen, ideally without the mash on top as it sometimes does not freeze well.

MARY'S EVERYDAY TIP

It is important for the mince to be cold before adding the mash; if it is hot, the mash will not be able to spread across the top properly and will mix in with the mince. By contrast, the mash spreads better when it's warm.

POULTRY

Chicken is such a versatile ingredient, and with a few extra herbs, spices or flavours can be transformed into something really special. Try my Chicken, Squash and Fennel Bake (page 125) for a speedy weeknight supper, or Griddled Chicken Carbonara (page 130) for a delicious Friday-night treat.

MARSALA MEDITERRANEAN CHICKEN THIGHS

This is a really lovely recipe for all the family – a dish to suit everyone. The sauce has enough depth and flavour for the grown-ups, while the creaminess makes it ideal for younger palates too, lifted by the freshness of the tomatoes and basil. It could be served with rice, or crusty bread and salad, or even mixed with pasta for the children. Just don't confuse Marsala wine with masala spice!

SERVES 4–6

COOK TIME:
30–35 MINUTES

25g (1oz) butter

2 tbsp olive oil

12 skinless and boneless chicken thighs

1 red onion, finely sliced

2 garlic cloves, crushed

2 tinned anchovies, chopped

150ml (5fl oz) Marsala wine (see tip)

150ml (5fl oz) chicken stock

1 tbsp cornflour

200g (7oz) cherry tomatoes

100g (4oz) black olives

150ml (5fl oz) double cream

Salt and freshly ground black pepper

1 handful of small basil leaves, to garnish

1. Heat the butter and olive oil in a large, deep frying pan and, when the butter has melted, sear the chicken thighs over a high heat for 3–4 minutes on each side until golden. You may need to do this in two batches for this number of chicken thighs. Remove from the pan and set aside.

2. Add the onion and garlic to the pan (no need to clean it first) and fry over a high heat for 2–3 minutes. Cover with a lid, lower the heat and cook for about 5 minutes or until soft. Add the anchovies, then stir in the Marsala and bring to the boil, allowing the wine to boil for a minute to cook out the alcohol before pouring in the stock.

3. Mix the cornflour with 1 tablespoon of cold water in a bowl to give a smooth paste (see tip). Whisk in about 150ml (5fl oz) of the liquid from the pan. Return to the pan and stir in. Bring the mixture to the boil and allow to bubble until thickened slightly. Season with salt and pepper.

4. Return the chicken thighs to the pan and bring back up to the boil. Cover again with the lid, then reduce the heat and simmer for about 10 minutes.

5. Add the tomatoes and olives and stir in well, before cooking for a further 5 minutes. Stir in the double cream and continue to cook for a few minutes.

6. Spoon into a warmed serving dish and sprinkle with the basil leaves.

PREPARE AHEAD

Can be made in advance up to the end of step 4. Reheat, adding the tomatoes, olives and cream as in step 5, then garnish with the basil to serve.

MARY'S EVERYDAY TIPS

A dry white sherry could be substituted for the Marsala.

Only add cold water to cornflour, not hot, or the paste will be lumpy.

CHICKEN THIGHS WITH GARLIC CREAM CHEESE

These are perfect for a casual supper. The garlicky cream cheese not only gives a lovely flavour but keeps the chicken very moist, while the paprika adds colour and aroma to the skin and the juices in the pan. You could use fresh herbs, such as parsley or chives, instead of the spring onions, if you liked.

SERVES 4–6

COOK TIME:
35 MINUTES

6 boneless chicken thighs, skin on (see tip)

1 tbsp runny honey

1 tbsp paprika

FOR THE FILLING

100g (4oz) full-fat cream cheese

3 spring onions, finely chopped

1 tbsp chopped basil

1 garlic clove, crushed

1 tbsp lemon juice

Salt and freshly ground black pepper

1. Preheat the oven to 200°C/180°C fan/Gas 6.

2. Place all the filling ingredients in a bowl, season with salt and pepper and mix until combined.

3. Place the chicken thighs on a board and use your fingers to carefully pull back the skin to form a pocket. Divide the mixture between the chicken thighs, spreading it evenly over the meat, then pull the skin back over and press around the edges to enclose the filling.

4. Arrange the stuffed chicken thighs in a roasting tin, drizzle over the honey and sprinkle with the paprika (see tip). Roast in the oven for about 35 minutes or until golden brown and cooked through.

5. Serve hot or save to eat cold, cut up into slices.

PREPARE AHEAD

Can be filled up to a day ahead. The filled thighs can be cooked up to a day ahead and eaten cold.

MARY'S EVERYDAY TIPS

If you can't find boneless chicken thighs with the skin on, buy ones on the bone and ask your butcher to remove the bones for you. Or you can slip the single bone out yourself, with a small, sharp knife.

The honey and paprika helps the skin of the chicken turn golden brown and crispy.

SPICED CHICKEN LEGS WITH ROASTED ONIONS

A really quick recipe to prepare, ideal for entertaining or for a family meal – great for teenagers! The chicken is full of flavour, with a touch of curry about it. It's also a highly versatile dish that could be served at any time of year – in the summer with new potatoes and salad, or in the winter with rice and hot vegetables.

SERVES 6

COOK TIME:
40–45 MINUTES

3 onions, sliced

6 chicken legs (drumsticks and thighs), skin on

Salt and freshly ground black pepper

FOR THE PASTE

2 tbsp chopped fresh root ginger

2 tbsp mango chutney

1 tbsp ground coriander

½ tsp Chinese five spice powder

½ fresh red chilli, deseeded and chopped

2 garlic cloves, sliced

2 tbsp sunflower oil

FOR THE SAUCE

100ml (3½fl oz) double cream

1 tsp mango chutney

1 tsp soy sauce

1 tbsp lemon juice

2 tsp cornflour

1. Preheat the oven to 200°C/180°C fan/Gas 6.

2. Place all the ingredients for the paste in a mini food processor and whizz until smooth.

3. Put the onions into the base of a small roasting or traybake tin. Arrange the chicken legs on top, spread the paste over the chicken and season with salt and pepper.

4. Roast in the oven for 40–45 minutes, basting halfway through the cooking time, until the chicken is golden brown and cooked through and the onions are soft. Remove the onions and chicken and set aside on a plate, loosely wrapped in foil to keep warm, while you make the sauce.

5. Strain the juices from the tin into a saucepan. Skim off the fat and discard (see tip), then add the cream to the pan and bring to the boil. Boil for 1 minute to reduce the liquid, then stir in the mango chutney, soy sauce and lemon juice.

6. Mix the cornflour with 1 tablespoon of cold water until smooth, then add to the sauce (see tip). Bring back up to the boil and stir until the sauce has thickened. Add the cooked onions and season with salt and pepper to taste.

7. Serve the chicken legs with the creamy sauce.

PREPARE AHEAD

The paste can be made up to a day ahead.

MARY'S EVERYDAY TIPS

If you prefer, you could use chicken breasts instead. They would work well in this recipe and take only 30 minutes to cook.

Wait for the juices to cool first, if you like; the fat will then float to the top, making it easier to skim off.

If the sauce is thick enough already, you may not need to add the cornflour.

CHICKEN, SQUASH AND FENNEL BAKE

This all-in-one dish would be perfect for a weekday supper for all the family. The squash and fennel contrast nicely with the moist, crispy chicken while the wine makes a flavoursome sauce, with added sweetness from the honey. Delicious!

SERVES 6

COOK TIME:
50–55 MINUTES

2 fennel bulbs, trimmed, core removed and each bulb cut into 6 wedges

1 red onion, cut into 6 wedges

1 butternut squash, peeled (see tip), deseeded and cut into 2cm (¾in) cubes (about 1kg/2lb 3oz prepared weight)

4 tbsp olive oil

2 garlic cloves, crushed

2 tbsp runny honey

6 boneless chicken breasts (about 175g/6oz each), skin on

½–1 tsp paprika

50g (2oz) Parmesan cheese, grated

150ml (5fl oz) white wine

1 tbsp finely chopped sage

Salt and freshly ground black pepper

1. Preheat the oven to 220°C/200°C fan/Gas 7.

2. Bring a large, deep saucepan of water to the boil, add the fennel and onion and parboil for about 5 minutes, then drain.

3. Scatter the parboiled vegetables and the squash over the base of a large roasting tin, drizzle with 2 tablespoons of the olive oil, season with salt and pepper and toss together. Place in the oven to roast for 15 minutes.

4. Meanwhile, mix the garlic with the honey and the remaining oil.

5. Remove the tin from the oven, sit the chicken breasts, skin side up, on top of the vegetables and spoon over the garlic and honey mixture. Sprinkle evenly with the paprika and Parmesan. Pour the white wine into the base of the tin and return to the oven for 30–35 minutes, until the chicken is cooked through and golden.

6. Scatter with the sage and serve piping hot.

PREPARE AHEAD

Assemble in the tin up to 4 hours ahead.

MARY'S EVERYDAY TIP

To save time, thin-skinned squashes can be roasted unpeeled; just wipe the skin and chop.

CHICKEN STIR-FRY WITH TERIYAKI SAUCE

Stir-fries are a family favourite as they are so quick and easy to knock up, using any vegetables you have to hand. This one has plenty of flavour, spicy from the soy and ginger but not hot, making it ideal for younger children.

SERVES 4–6

COOK TIME:
10–15 MINUTES,
PLUS MARINATING

2 skinless and boneless
   chicken breasts, sliced
   into thin strips

200g (7oz) fine egg
   noodles (see tip)

2 tbsp olive oil

150g (5oz) baby corn,
   sliced in half lengthways

200g (7oz) mangetout,
   sliced in half lengthways

4 spring onions, chopped

100g (4oz) bean
   sprouts, rinsed

**FOR THE TERIYAKI
SAUCE**

90ml (3fl oz) soy sauce

4 tbsp sesame oil

4 tbsp sweet sherry

4cm (1½in) knob of fresh root
   ginger, peeled and grated
   (see tip on page 61)

1 garlic clove, crushed

Salt and freshly ground
   black pepper

1. Place all the ingredients for the sauce in a bowl and stir to combine. Add the chicken strips, season with salt and pepper and toss together. Set aside to marinate for a minimum of 30 minutes.

2. Cook the noodles in boiling salted water according to the packet instructions. Drain well and rinse in cold water.

3. Heat 1 tablespoon of the oil in a wok or deep frying pan. Remove the chicken from the marinade and fry over a high heat for 3–4 minutes on each side until golden all over and just cooked through. Remove with a slotted spoon and set aside.

4. Add the remaining tablespoon of oil to the pan, tip in the baby corn, mangetout, spring onions and bean sprouts and fry over a high heat for 3–4 minutes.

5. Return the noodles and chicken to the pan, pour in the sauce and toss to combine over the heat until piping hot. Tip into a warmed platter to serve.

PREPARE AHEAD

The chicken can be marinated in the sauce up to a day ahead. It can be pan-fried up to 3 hours ahead and reheated with the freshly cooked noodles and vegetables to serve.

MARY'S EVERYDAY TIP

Different brands of noodles have different cooking times, so do check the packet before cooking, and look out for wholewheat noodles for a healthier option.

CHICKEN DIJON

So simple to prepare, this will be a big hit with young and old alike. A classic dish, it works well as a family meal or to serve guests. The rich and creamy sauce has a little kick from the mustard, but not enough to put off any fussy eaters. Serve with mash and a green veg, and supper is sorted!

SERVES 6

COOK TIME:
35–40 MINUTES

25g (1oz) butter

2 tbsp olive oil

6 small skinless and boneless chicken breasts (about 150g/5oz each)

2 banana shallots, finely sliced

2 garlic cloves, crushed

300ml (10fl oz) white wine

2 tbsp Dijon mustard (see tip)

300ml (10fl oz) pouring double cream

Salt and freshly ground black pepper

A few finely snipped chives, to garnish

1. Heat the butter and olive oil in a deep frying pan. Season each chicken breast with salt and pepper, and when the butter has melted, brown over a high heat for 3–4 minutes on each side. Once browned, remove the chicken from the pan and set aside.

2. Add the shallots to the pan and fry over a high heat for 1 minute. Add the garlic, then cover with a lid, lower the heat and gently cook for 5–10 minutes or until the shallots are soft and lightly browned.

3. Pour in the wine and bring to the boil, stirring, for about 5 minutes until the liquid has reduced by about two-thirds. Add the mustard and cream and boil for 3–4 minutes until the sauce has thickened slightly. Season with salt and pepper, return the chicken breasts and any juices to the pan, cover again with the lid, then lower the heat and simmer for about 15 minutes until cooked through and tender.

4. Serve each chicken breast whole or carved into three, with the sauce spooned over and sprinkled with chives.

PREPARE AHEAD

Can be fully made up to a day ahead and reheated to serve before garnishing with the chives.

MARY'S EVERYDAY TIP

Mustard can vary quite a bit, so check the strength of the mustard before you use it and taste the sauce before adding the chicken in step 3.

GRIDDLED CHICKEN CARBONARA

Here I've given pasta carbonara a lovely twist by serving it with pieces of chargrilled chicken breast on top to make a more substantial meal. The recipe is very straightforward, but timing is quite tight. The pasta needs to remain hot to gently cook the egg sauce, so once you've put the pan of water on to boil the pasta, you'll need to immediately start cooking the chicken. The whole process should take around 15 minutes.

SERVES 6

COOK TIME:
15 MINUTES

350g (12oz) dried tagliatelle

1 tbsp oil

3 chicken breasts (about 175g/6oz each), each cut into four

2 egg yolks (see tip)

150ml (5fl oz) pouring double cream

75g (3oz) Parmesan, finely grated, plus extra to serve

175g (6oz) dry-cured streaky bacon, finely sliced

2 garlic cloves, crushed

Salt and freshly ground black pepper

1 handful of small basil leaves, to garnish

1. Heat a large saucepan of salted water, then add the tagliatelle and cook according to the packet instructions. Drain in a colander, reserving 90ml (3fl oz) of the cooking water, then return the drained pasta to the warm pan.

2. As soon as you've put the pan of water on to boil for the pasta, place a large griddle pan (see tips) on a high heat and when hot, add the oil. Fry the chicken pieces for about 3–4 minutes on each side or until cooked through and golden. Remove from the pan and set aside to keep warm.

3. While the chicken is cooking, place the egg yolks, cream and Parmesan in a bowl, season well with salt and pepper and stir until combined.

4. Place the bacon in the griddle pan and fry for about 5 minutes until crisp and golden. Add the garlic and fry for another minute. Transfer the griddled bacon and garlic to the drained tagliatelle in the saucepan, pour in the reserved pasta water and the cream mixture and toss together well.

5. Add a portion of the pasta to each plate, twisting some of the tagliatelle around a fork to form a nest. Sit two pieces of chicken on top in a cross and sprinkle with basil leaves and extra Parmesan.

MARY'S EVERYDAY TIPS

This recipe is a good way to use up leftover egg yolks – for example, after making meringues such as the Rainbow Meringues on page 266. Even if you're not using the egg whites straight away, they freeze beautifully; it's worth keeping a stock of them in the freezer.

A large, deep frying pan can be used instead of a griddle pan, but it won't give those lovely chargrilled marks.

Try not to crowd the pan – cook in batches to ensure that the chicken pieces each have the griddle marks on them. Note, however, that cooking the chicken in two batches will affect the overall timing; you'll need to cook the chicken first and keep it warm while you boil the pasta and prepare the sauce.

PANANG CHICKEN AND RICE STIR-FRY

A wonderfully handy recipe for an everyday midweek supper – one to rival any takeaway! The delicious mixture of honey-coated chicken with tender rice and stir-fried vegetables is a meal in itself, though you could serve it with prawn crackers for a weekend treat. This is also great for using up any veg that you have in the fridge – just remember to cut them into small pieces to cook with the other vegetables.

SERVES 4–6

COOK TIME:
25 MINUTES

225g (8oz) long-grain rice

2 tbsp olive oil

2 skinless and boneless chicken breasts, sliced into very thin strips

1 tbsp runny honey

1 onion, finely chopped

1 red pepper, deseeded and finely diced

2 celery sticks, finely diced

1 medium courgette, finely diced

2cm (¾in) knob of fresh root ginger, peeled and finely grated (see tip on page 61)

2 garlic cloves, crushed

1 tbsp medium curry powder

3 tbsp soy sauce

1 tbsp sweet chilli sauce

Juice of ½ lime

Salt and freshly ground black pepper

4–6 lime wedges, to serve

1. Cook the rice in boiling salted water (see tip) according to the packet instructions, then drain well, rinse in boiling water from the kettle and set aside to drain.

2. Heat the oil in a wok or wide-based frying pan, season the chicken strips with salt and pepper and add to the pan. Drizzle with honey (see tip) and stir-fry over a high heat for 2–3 minutes, turning until golden and just cooked, then remove with a slotted spoon and set aside.

3. Tip in the onion and vegetables, and stir-fry for 4–5 minutes. Add the ginger, garlic and curry powder and fry for another minute, stirring well.

4. Add the cooked rice with the soy sauce, chilli sauce and lime juice. Toss together until piping hot, season with salt and pepper to taste (see tip), and return the chicken to the pan.

5. Remove from the heat and spoon into warmed bowls to serve, with lime wedges.

PREPARE AHEAD

The rice can be cooked up to 6 hours ahead and kept in the fridge, ready to add.

MARY'S EVERYDAY TIPS

Cook the rice in plenty of water so that it doesn't stick together.

The honey helps the chicken go brown quickly and therefore prevents it from being cooked for too long and becoming dry.

Soy sauce can be a little salty, so go steady with extra seasoning.

CHICKEN BREASTS WITH RED PEPPER AND GOAT'S CHEESE

Rich goat's cheese with sweet red peppers and onion marmalade make a classic combination for topping chicken breasts. It keeps the chicken very moist and adds an intensely sweet yet savoury flavour, while the panko breadcrumbs give a lovely, crisp crust. Serve with new potatoes and a green vegetable.

SERVES 6

COOK TIME:
30 MINUTES

2 tbsp olive oil

2 small red peppers, deseeded and thinly sliced

3–4 tbsp onion marmalade or caramelised onion chutney

200g (7oz) rindless full-fat firm goat's cheese (see tip), cut into small cubes

6 skinless and boneless chicken breasts (about 150g/5oz each)

25g (1oz) panko breadcrumbs (see tip on page 108)

½–1 tsp paprika

Salt and freshly ground black pepper

1. Preheat the oven 200°C/180°C fan/Gas 6 and line the base of a roasting tin with baking paper.

2. Heat the oil in a non-stick frying pan, add the peppers and fry over a high heat for about 5 minutes or until soft and tinged brown. Tip into a bowl to cool, then stir in the onion marmalade/chutney and the goat's cheese and season well with salt and pepper.

3. Arrange the chicken breasts in the prepared tin and season with salt and pepper. Spoon the goat's cheese mixture on top of the chicken pieces, then sprinkle with the breadcrumbs and paprika.

4. Bake in the oven for about 25 minutes or until the chicken is golden on top and cooked through, the juices running clear when the chicken is pierced with a knife.

5. Serve the topped chicken pieces hot with the juices from the pan poured over.

PREPARE AHEAD

Can be assembled up to 6 hours ahead.

MARY'S EVERYDAY TIP

If a milder cheese is preferred, use cream cheese instead.

CHICKEN VALENCIA

Simple but tasty and with lots of flavoursome sauce, this is a casserole that you will come back to again and again. You could make it with chicken breasts, too, which would reduce the oven cooking time to 25 minutes.

SERVES 4-6

COOK TIME:
55 MINUTES

2 tbsp sunflower oil

8 chicken thighs on the bone, skin removed

6 rashers of smoked streaky bacon, thinly sliced

2 onions, thinly sliced

3 garlic cloves, crushed

25g (1oz) plain flour

300ml (10fl oz) white wine

1 x 400g tin of chopped tomatoes

1 tbsp muscovado sugar

400g (14oz) button mushrooms, sliced

1 tbsp chopped thyme leaves

Salt and freshly ground black pepper

1. Preheat the oven to 160°C/140°C fan/Gas 3.

2. Heat 1 tablespoon of the oil in a large, deep ovenproof pan or casserole dish with a lid. Season the chicken thighs with salt and pepper, then add to the pan and brown over a high heat for 2–3 minutes on each side until golden all over. Remove, cover with foil and set aside.

3. Add the bacon and onions to the pan (no need to clean it first) and fry for 3–4 minutes over a high heat until the bacon is crispy. Add the garlic and fry for a further 30 seconds.

4. Measure the flour into a bowl, then add the wine little by little and whisk into a smooth paste. Add to the pan with the tomatoes (see tip) and sugar and stir in well. Bring to the boil, then return the chicken and any juices to the pan and bring back up to the boil, stirring. Cover with the lid and cook in the oven for 45 minutes or until the chicken is tender and cooked through.

5. Shortly before the chicken is ready, heat the remaining oil in a frying pan, add the mushrooms and fry for 3–4 minutes until golden and just cooked. Add the mushrooms to the casserole and stir in the thyme.

6. Serve the casserole hot with mash and a green vegetable such as kale.

PREPARE AHEAD

Can be made up to 2 days ahead and reheated to serve.

FREEZE *Freezes well without the mushrooms.*

MARY'S EVERYDAY TIP

Rinse the chopped tomatoes tin out with a little of the wine mixture and tip into the pan to use up every drop.

CRISPY-SKINNED DUCK BREASTS WITH PAK CHOI AND PINEAPPLE SAUCE

Delicious duck breasts cooked in an Oriental style with crunchy stir-fried vegetables and a distinctive sweet and sour sauce. The duck should be served pink, so the timings below are for meat that is pink in the middle. Duck fat can be very thick and unpleasant to eat unless it's really crisp, so I've made sure that it's fully rendered first. The duck breasts are then cooked on a high heat to ensure the skin is nice and crispy while the meat stays beautifully moist.

SERVES 6

COOK TIME:
30 MINUTES, PLUS RESTING

6 duck breasts (about 200g/7oz each – see tip), skin on

10 spring onions, sliced on the diagonal

2 Romano red peppers, deseeded and thickly sliced

500g (1lb 2oz) pak choi, green and white parts separated and cut into very thick slices

FOR THE SAUCE

300ml (10fl oz) pineapple juice

1½ tbsp cornflour

2 tbsp soy sauce

2 tbsp white wine vinegar

50g (2oz) light muscovado sugar

1 tbsp sweet chilli sauce

1 tsp grated fresh root ginger (see tip on page 61)

Salt and freshly ground black pepper

1. Using a sharp knife, score the skin of the duck breasts. Put the duck, skin side down, into a frying pan large enough to hold all six duck breasts. Place over a medium heat to allow the fat to slowly render down; tip off the fat as it melts (see tip). This will take 10–15 minutes, depending on the thickness of the skin.

2. While the duck fat is being rendered, make the sauce. Pour the pineapple juice into a saucepan, add the cornflour and whisk until smooth. Add the remaining ingredients for the sauce to the pan and stir over a medium heat until smooth and thickened. Season to taste with salt and pepper and keep warm over a low heat.

3. When there is just a thin layer of fat remaining in the frying pan, raise the heat a little, turn the duck breasts over and fry for 8–10 minutes. Turn the duck breasts over again, skin side down, then raise the heat to the highest level and push down each breast in the pan to crisp the fat. Once golden brown and crisp, set aside on a plate to rest for 5 minutes.

4. Remove all but 1 tablespoon of fat from the pan, then add the spring onions, red peppers and the white parts of the pak choi and briskly stir-fry over a high heat for about 3 minutes. Add the green parts of the pak choi, season with salt and pepper and cook for 1 minute until wilted.

5. Carve the duck into thick slices on the diagonal and serve on individual plates with the vegetables and hot sauce.

PREPARE AHEAD

The duck fat can be rendered up to 6 hours ahead, the duck breasts pan-fried to serve.

The sauce can be made up to 2 days ahead and reheated.

MARY'S EVERYDAY TIPS

Buy duck breasts that are all the same size so they cook at the same rate.

Keep the rendered duck fat for roasting potatoes.

FISH

Fish is a lovely light alternative to meat, and usually requires only a little preparation. Most varieties combine beautifully with other flavours, to make for fragrant dishes that will please the whole family. Seafood makes for an excellent midweek supper, such as my Fragrant Light Prawn Curry (page 155) or Golden Fried Crab and Basil Spaghetti (page 164).

VERY POSH FISHCAKES

These both look and taste amazing. When you cut into them, a wonderful cheesy sauce oozes out, which means no extra sauce is needed. Serve with a few dressed lamb's lettuce leaves.

MAKES 4 FISHCAKES

COOK TIME:
40 MINUTES,
PLUS COOLING

325g (11oz) floury potatoes
  (about 1 large), peeled
  and cubed

325g (11oz) undyed
  smoked haddock fillets

1 tbsp sunflower oil

A knob of butter

Salt and freshly ground
  black pepper

4 lemon wedges, to serve

**FOR THE
FONDANT SAUCE**

15g (½oz) butter

15g (½oz) plain flour

160ml (5fl oz) milk

½ tsp Dijon mustard

½ tbsp lemon juice

25g (1oz) Parmesan
  cheese, grated

2 tbsp chopped parsley

**FOR THE BREADCRUMB
COATING**

1 egg

3 tbsp plain flour

About 75g (3oz) fine panko
  breadcrumbs (see tip)

1. Preheat the oven 200°C/180°C fan/Gas 6.

2. Cook the potatoes in boiling salted water for about 15 minutes or until tender, then drain and mash well before setting aside to cool.

3. To cook the haddock, arrange the fillets, skin side up, on a sheet of foil and fold over the fish to make a parcel. Place on a baking tray and bake in the oven for about 15 minutes or until just cooked. Open the foil and peel the skin from each of the fillets, then set aside in the tin to cool in the juices. Leave the oven switched on and place a baking sheet inside to get very hot.

4. When the fish is cold, remove from the tin (reserving the juices) and flake large pieces into a bowl (see tip). Add the mash, mix gently to combine and season with salt and pepper. Chill in the fridge while you make the sauce.

5. Melt the 15g (½oz) of butter in a small saucepan, add the 15g (½oz) of flour and whisk over a medium heat for 2–3 minutes until smooth. Heat the milk in a separate pan, then gradually whisk into the butter and flour roux until you have a thick smooth sauce. Add the mustard, lemon juice, Parmesan and parsley, along with 2 tablespoons of the reserved fish cooking juices. Tip into a bowl and leave to cool for 15 minutes.

6. Divide the fish mixture into quarters and shape into four even-sized balls. Using your thumbs, make a deep well in the centre of each ball and spoon in thick cooled sauce until it comes to within 1cm (½in) of the top. Push some of the fish mixture on top so the cheese sauce is encased within the ball, then place on a board and press down a little to flatten into a fishcake (see tips).

7. Beat the egg for the coating in a shallow bowl, sprinkle the flour on to a plate and add the breadcrumbs to another plate. Coat each fishcake all over, first in the flour, then in the egg and finally the breadcrumbs, pressing the breadcrumbs in well and up the sides to ensure the fishcake is fully covered. Set aside on a plate until ready to cook.

Recipe continues overleaf

8. Heat the oil and butter in a large frying pan, add the fishcakes and carefully fry over a medium heat for 2–3 minutes on each side until golden all over. Transfer to the hot baking sheet and slide into the oven to cook for 15 minutes or until piping hot inside.

9. Serve hot with the lemon wedges.

PREPARE AHEAD

Can be made the day before. Pan-fry up to 8 hours ahead and cook in the oven (preheated as in step 1) for 30 minutes to serve.

FREEZE *Freezes well uncooked.*

MARY'S EVERYDAY TIPS

Try to keep the fish in fairly chunky flakes, so the fishcakes have a good texture.

Panko breadcrumbs are my favourite as they stay crisp during cooking and give a lovely texture. Different brands vary in coarseness, however, and it's best to use very fine breadcrumbs for this recipe. If yours are coarse, place in a resealable freezer bag and bash with a rolling pin to make them finer.

You may prefer to shape the fishcakes using wet hands – this makes it easier to handle the mash. It can be tricky to re-shape the balls once they are filled with sauce, hence not filling them quite to the top.

If you have any of the fondant sauce left over, warm through in a small milk pan and serve on the side.

FISH AND CHIPS WITH TARTARE SAUCE

Try making your own fish and chips for an everyday treat – far tastier and so much healthier (no deep-frying!) than a takeaway. I've used tail-end cod fillets here, which are thinner and cook more quickly. Panko breadcrumbs give great texture, and most supermarkets stock them, but you could use ready-prepared standard breadcrumbs otherwise, or make your own (see tip on page 159).

SERVES 6

COOK TIME:
30 MINUTES

50g (2oz) plain flour

100g (4oz) panko
  breadcrumbs
  (see tip on page 159)

2 eggs, beaten

6 x 150g (5oz) tail-end
  pieces of cod fillet,
  skinned (see tip)

1kg (2lb 3oz) medium
  Maris Piper or King
  Edward potatoes

105ml (3½fl oz) sunflower oil

Salt and freshly ground
  black pepper

Parsley sprigs, to garnish

Lemon wedges, to serve

**FOR THE
TARTARE SAUCE**

90g (3½oz) mayonnaise

2 tbsp double cream

2 tbsp sweet gherkins,
  very finely chopped

2 tbsp chopped capers

Juice of ½ lemon

1 tbsp snipped chives

1 tbsp chopped parsley

A pinch of sugar

1. Measure the flour and breadcrumbs on to two separate plates and beat the eggs in a shallow bowl.

2. Season the cod fillets on both sides with salt and pepper (or season the flour on the plate, if you prefer). Dip each fillet first into the flour, then the egg and then the breadcrumbs, pressing the crumbs on to the fish so that each piece is evenly coated on both sides. Transfer the breadcrumbed fillets to a plate or tray, cover and chill in the fridge for 30 minutes to firm up.

3. Meanwhile, preheat the oven to 220°C/200°C fan/Gas 7 and line three baking sheets (one large and two standard-sized ones) with baking paper.

4. Peel the potatoes and slice into thick chips. Place in a resealable freezer bag, add 3 tablespoons of the sunflower oil and toss together to coat the potatoes evenly in oil. Tip on to the two smaller baking sheets in an even layer. Place on separate shelves towards the top of the oven and roast for about 15 minutes, then turn the chips over and swap the trays round on the shelves so they cook evenly. Roast for a further 15 minutes or until golden and tender.

5. While the chips are roasting, start cooking the fish. Pour enough of the oil (about 2 tablespoons) into a large frying pan so it forms a thin layer on the bottom and set over a high heat (see tip). Add the cod fillets and fry on each side for about 3 minutes or until golden. Do this in two batches, adding the remaining oil for the second batch, and sit on kitchen paper to drain for a minute.

6. Shortly before the potatoes have finished cooking, transfer the fish to the large baking sheet and cook in the oven for 5–6 minutes or until cooked through.

Recipe continues overleaf

7. To make the tartare sauce, mix all the ingredients together in a bowl and season with salt and pepper.

8. Remove the fish and chips from the oven. Garnish each fillet with a sprig of parsley and serve piping hot with the chips, tartare sauce and lemon wedges.

PREPARE AHEAD

The fish can be pan-fried ahead and then cooked in the oven for 10 minutes from cold. Alternatively, the cod can be coated in the breadcrumbs and kept in the fridge for 2 hours before cooking. This will also help the coating to firm up and hold together.

The sauce can be made up to 3 days ahead and kept in the fridge.

MARY'S EVERYDAY TIPS

Ask your fishmonger to skin the fish for you, or see the tip on page 159 for doing it yourself.

For best results when frying the fish, fry a breadcrumb first. If it turns golden, the oil is hot enough for cooking the cod.

MARINATED HARISSA PRAWNS WITH SPICED RICE

This is a fresh and healthy dish, full of lovely contrasting flavours and textures. The harissa has a rounded taste that's not too spicy. Buy large, fresh prawns with the shell on but remove the shell on the tail before cooking, just leaving the head on. This looks impressive and makes the prawns easier to eat, although you may want to provide a finger bowl for sticky fingers!

SERVES 6

COOK TIME:
20–25 MINUTES

18 raw king prawns, shell on

1–2 tbsp oil, for frying (see tip)

1 tbsp chopped parsley, to garnish

FOR THE RICE SALAD

250g (9oz) basmati or long-grain rice

250g (9oz) chargrilled red peppers in oil (from a jar), drained and chopped into 1cm (½in) pieces

175g (6oz) chargrilled artichoke hearts in oil (from a jar), sliced into 1cm (½in) pieces

8 ready-to-eat dried apricots, snipped into 1cm (½in) pieces

1 bunch of parsley, chopped

Salt and freshly ground black pepper

FOR THE SPICED DRESSING

85ml (3fl oz) oil (see tip)

Juice of ½ lemon

1 small garlic clove, crushed

2 tsp ground cumin

2 tsp ground coriander

1 tsp harissa paste

1 tsp sugar

FOR THE MARINADE

1 tbsp harissa paste

1 large garlic clove, crushed

1 tbsp oil (see tip)

1. Cook the rice in boiling salted water according to the packet instructions (usually 12–15 minutes), then drain, rinse and set aside in the colander to cool quickly and dry out. When the rice is cold, tip into a bowl. Add all the remaining ingredients for the rice salad, seasoning with salt and pepper, and stir to combine.

2. Mix together all the ingredients for the dressing, pour over the rice salad and stir in.

3. Remove the shell and legs from the body of each of the prawns, leaving the head on. De-vein the prawns. Place the harissa paste, garlic and oil in a bowl and stir to combine, then add the prawns, season with salt and pepper and toss until well coated. Leave for a minimum of 15 minutes to marinate.

4. Heat 1 tablespoon of oil in a frying pan, add the prawns and fry over a high heat for 3–4 minutes until pink and curled up, turning halfway through the cooking time. Cook in batches if needed. Remove from the pan and set aside to rest for a few minutes. Add the rice to the hot pan (you may need to add a little more oil to the pan first) and toss over a high heat for 3–4 minutes or until piping hot.

5. Transfer the rice to a serving plate with the prawns arranged on top. Sprinkle with parsley, if you like.

PREPARE AHEAD

The prawns can be left to marinate up to 6 hours ahead.

The rice salad can be made up to a day ahead and kept in the fridge. Pour over the dressing up to 30 minutes before heating through to serve. (Rice must be cooled quickly, stored in the fridge and reheated thoroughly.)

MARY'S EVERYDAY TIP

Reserve the oil from the artichokes and red peppers, using 85ml (3fl oz) for the dressing (topped up with olive oil, if needed), 1 tablespoon for the marinade and 1–2 tablespoons for frying the prawns and rice.

YUZU SALMON WITH BUTTERED LEEKS

A quick everyday recipe, but good enough to impress friends too. It can be prepared ahead as well, making it a great option for entertaining. The dish has a wonderfully fresh citrus flavour from the yuzu juice (see tip), offsetting the richness of the salmon, and with a touch of heat from the ginger and chilli. When mixed with the radishes, the yuzu juice effectively pickles them, bringing out the beautiful colour.

SERVES 4

COOK TIME:
25–30 MINUTES

25g (1oz) butter

4 small leeks, finely sliced

4 x 125g (4½oz) salmon
  fillets, skinned
  (see tip on page 159)

FOR THE DRESSING

2cm (¾in) knob of fresh root
  ginger, peeled and grated
  (see tip on page 61)

2 garlic cloves, crushed

1 small fresh red chilli,
  deseeded and very
  finely chopped

2 tbsp yuzu juice (see tip)

4 tbsp sunflower oil

Salt and freshly ground
  black pepper

TO GARNISH

Leaves from 1 small
  bunch of coriander

3–4 pink radishes (see tip),
  thinly shaved with
  a vegetable peeler

1. Preheat the oven to 200°C/180°C fan/Gas 6.

2. Heat the butter in a large frying pan and when it has melted, add the leeks and fry over a high heat for 2–3 minutes. Cover the pan with a lid, lower the heat and sweat for 10–15 minutes or until soft but not browned. Tip into an open ovenproof dish or roasting tin.

3. Add the ginger and garlic to a bowl with the chilli, yuzu juice and oil. Season with salt and pepper and stir to combine, reserving 2 tablespoons of the dressing in a separate bowl.

4. Sit the salmon fillets on top of the leeks, season with salt and pepper and carefully spoon the dressing over the salmon so that the pieces of ginger and chilli rest on top of the salmon. Bake, uncovered, in the oven for 12–15 minutes or until the fish is just cooked through.

5. Toss the coriander leaves and radishes in the reserved 2 tablespoons of dressing. Serve a spoonful of leeks on each plate with a salmon fillet on top and a pile of dressed coriander and radishes on top of each fillet.

PREPARE AHEAD

The fish and the leeks can be assembled up to 6 hours ahead, ready to go in the oven. Increase the oven time to 20 minutes and pour over the dressing just before cooking.

Leftovers will make a lovely cold salad for the following day.

MARY'S EVERYDAY TIPS

Yuzu juice has been hailed as a new superfood because of its high levels of vitamin C. The yuzu is a Japanese citrus fruit, varying from green to yellow, depending on how ripe it is, with a tart flavour that resembles a mixture of lemon, lime and mandarin. Used for years in Asian cooking, the yuzu is now widely available in shops in the UK in the form of the fresh fruit or juice. The bottled juice keeps well in the fridge.

Use red radishes if pink are unavailable.

FIVE SPICE SALMON STIR-FRY

Quick, healthy and full of flavour, this dish is tailor-made for a busy weekday supper. The salmon can be marinated in advance, making it an easy, nutritious meal to whip up for the family after school or work.

SERVES 6

COOK TIME:
20 MINUTES

300g (11oz) salmon fillet, skinned (see tip on page 159)

175g (6oz) medium egg noodles

2 tbsp olive oil

1 onion, sliced

1 red pepper, deseeded and finely sliced

2 large carrots, peeled and sliced into thin batons

100g (4oz) frozen peas

200g (7oz) bean sprouts, rinsed

Juice of 1 lime

Salt

Basil leaves, to garnish

FOR THE MARINADE

1 tbsp soy sauce

1 tbsp sweet chilli sauce

1 tsp Chinese five spice powder

FOR THE SAUCE

½ fresh red chilli, deseeded and finely chopped

2cm (¾in) knob of fresh root ginger, peeled and finely grated (see tip on page 61)

3 tbsp soy sauce

2 tbsp sweet chilli sauce

Juice of ½ lime

1. Slice the salmon fillet into 3cm (1¼in) squares. Mix the marinade ingredients together in a bowl, add the salmon squares and toss to coat. Leave to marinate for 10 minutes.

2. Meanwhile, make the sauce. Place the chilli and ginger in a bowl with the soy sauce, chilli sauce and lime juice and mix together.

3. Cook the noodles in boiling salted water, according to the packet instructions. Drain and then refresh in cold water to stop the noodles from cooking any further.

4. Heat half the oil in a large frying pan or wok over a high heat, add the salmon with the marinade and carefully toss for 3–4 minutes until just cooked (see tip). Remove with a slotted spoon and transfer to a plate.

5. Heat the remaining oil in the pan (no need to clean it first), add the onion, red pepper and carrots and fry over a high heat for 3 minutes. Tip in the peas and toss until thawed. Add the cooked noodles to the pan, pour over the sauce and stir-fry for 2 minutes.

6. Return the salmon to the pan, add the bean sprouts and toss for a few minutes until piping hot. Add the lime juice and serve piping hot with a few basil leaves to garnish.

PREPARE AHEAD

Leave the salmon to marinate up to 4 hours ahead and cook to serve.

The sauce can be mixed together up to a day ahead.

MARY'S EVERYDAY TIP

Be careful not to break up the salmon when tossing – you want large visible cubes of fish in the finished dish.

FRAGRANT LIGHT PRAWN CURRY

Curries come in many forms, with a whole range of different tastes, textures and levels of heat. This is lighter, milder and more delicate than many, with lots of delicious fresh flavours.

SERVES 4–6

COOK TIME:
20 MINUTES

1 x 400g tin of full-fat coconut milk

150ml (5fl oz) fish or vegetable stock

Juice of 1 lime

4 lime leaves

1½ tbsp cornflour

100g (4oz) baby corn, sliced in half lengthways

100g (4oz) sugar snap peas, sliced in half lengthways

100g (4oz) baby pak choi, leaves separated

350g (12oz) raw tiger prawns, peeled

FOR THE CURRY PASTE

1/2 fresh red chilli, deseeded and chopped

2 garlic cloves, crushed

2cm (¾in) knob of fresh root ginger, peeled and finely grated (see tip on page 61)

1 lemon grass stalk (outer leaves removed), chopped

2 shallots, chopped

2 tbsp chopped coriander

1 tbsp Thai fish sauce

1 tbsp dark muscovado sugar

Salt

TO GARNISH

1 tbsp chopped coriander

1/2 fresh red chilli, deseeded and chopped

1. First make the curry paste. Add half the red chilli to a food processor with the garlic, ginger, lemon grass, shallots, coriander, fish sauce, sugar and 2 teaspoons of salt, and whizz into a thick paste.

2. Add the paste to a medium saucepan and cook gently for 2–3 minutes, without allowing it to brown. Pour in the coconut milk, stock (see tip) and lime juice, add the lime leaves and bring to the boil, stirring all the while.

3. Measure the cornflour into a bowl with 2 tablespoons of cold water (see tip) and stir until smooth. Add to the pan, bring back to the boil, stirring continuously, until the sauce begins to thicken very slightly.

4. In a separate pan, cook the baby corn and sugar snap peas in boiling salted water for 2 minutes, then drain and refresh in cold water.

5. Add the pak choi and prawns to the curry, with the blanched baby corn and sugar snap peas, bring back up to the boil and cook for 2–3 minutes or until the pak choi has wilted and the prawns are pink.

6. Remove the lime leaves and serve in warmed bowls, sprinkled with the coriander and remaining chopped chilli.

PREPARE AHEAD

The baby corn and sugar snap peas can be blanched in advance and refreshed in cold water.

MARY'S EVERYDAY TIP

To get every last bit of the flavoursome curry paste out of the food processor, use some of the stock to rinse around the goblet before pouring it into the pan with the rest of the stock.

SMOKED HADDOCK AND CAULIFLOWER GRATIN

Think of fish pie and cauliflower cheese and combine the two – delicious! Using a very simple sauce consisting of thickened cream, with the cheese layered into the dish, means it's quick to prepare too. It makes a comforting meal in itself, though you could serve it with warm crusty bread, if you liked.

SERVES 6

COOK TIME:
30–35 MINUTES

Butter, for greasing

350g (12oz) potatoes (about 2 small/medium), peeled and cut into 2cm (¾in) cubes

1 medium cauliflower, broken into small florets

1 heaped tbsp cornflour

300ml (10fl oz) pouring double cream

100g (4oz) Gruyère cheese, coarsely grated

2 tbsp chopped parsley

2 tbsp snipped chives

500g (1lb 2oz) undyed smoked haddock fillets, skinned (see tip below and on page 159) and cut into six large pieces

Paprika, for dusting

Salt and freshly ground black pepper

1. You will need a 2½–3-litre (4½–5-pint) wide-based, shallow ovenproof dish. Preheat the oven to 200°C/180°C fan/Gas 6 and grease the dish with butter.

2. Put the potato cubes into a large saucepan, cover with water, add a little salt and bring to the boil. Boil for about 4 minutes, then add the cauliflower florets and boil for a further 4 minutes. Drain well.

3. Tip the potatoes and cauliflower into the prepared dish and season with salt and pepper. Measure the cornflour into a bowl, pour in the cream, add some salt and pepper and stir to combine.

4. Scatter half the cheese over the cauliflower and potato in the dish. Sprinkle over the herbs, then add the pieces of haddock so that they cover the top in an even layer. Pour the cream mixture all over the top and in between the cracks. Scatter with the remaining cheese and dust with a little paprika.

5. Bake in the oven for 20–25 minutes or until golden and bubbling.

PREPARE AHEAD

Can be assembled up to 6 hours ahead and kept in the fridge. Bring to room temperature before cooking, or cook slightly longer until golden and bubbling.

MARY'S EVERYDAY TIP

Don't buy the yellow-dyed smoked haddock, as it is not a natural colouring.

CRUSTED CRAB AND COD FILLET WITH CHIVE LEMON SAUCE

Tender pieces of cod with a crunchy golden topping and a rich, tangy sauce – this makes an impressive supper dish. Use fresh white crabmeat, if you can, though tinned would be a good alternative. The cod fillets should be the same thickness as each other, ideally, so they cook in the same amount of time. You can ask your fishmonger to skin them, or see my tip below for skinning them yourself.

SERVES 6

COOK TIME:
15–18 MINUTES

6 x 150g (5oz) thick cod
  fillets, skinned

Salt and freshly ground
  black pepper

FOR THE TOPPING

300g (11oz) fresh
  white crabmeat

3 tbsp full-fat mayonnaise

Juice of ½ lemon

2 tbsp snipped chives

A dash of Tabasco sauce

FOR THE CRUST

50g (2oz) fine white
  breadcrumbs (see tip)

25g (1oz) Parmesan
  cheese, grated

Paprika, for sprinkling

**FOR THE CHIVE
LEMON SAUCE**

4 tbsp full-fat mayonnaise

200g (7oz) full-fat
  crème fraîche

Juice of ½ lemon

3 tbsp snipped chives

A dash of Tabasco sauce,
  to taste

1. Preheat the oven to 200°C/180°C fan/Gas 6 and line a large baking sheet with non-stick baking paper.

2. Season the cod fillets with salt and pepper and arrange on the prepared baking sheet, tucking any thin tail-end pieces underneath each of the fillets, so they look tidy and cook more evenly.

3. To make the topping, add the crabmeat to a bowl with the mayonnaise, lemon juice, chives and Tabasco sauce. Season with salt and pepper and stir to combine.

4. Divide the mixture into six and spread evenly on top of each fillet. Mix the breadcrumbs and Parmesan together in a bowl and sprinkle on top, pressing carefully into the crab mixture. Sprinkle with a little paprika.

5. Bake in the oven for 15–18 minutes until the cod fillets are cooked through and lightly golden and crunchy on top.

6. Combine all the ingredients for the sauce, season and serve with the cod.

PREPARE AHEAD

The cod can be assembled with the topping up to 6 hours ahead and kept in the fridge until ready to cook.

The sauce can be made up to 2 days ahead and stored in the fridge.

MARY'S EVERYDAY TIPS

To skin a fish fillet, place it skin down on a board. With a large sharp knife, cut through the flesh at the tail end, but stop at the skin. Holding the small end flap of skin firmly with one hand, slide the knife between the flesh and the skin, working it back and forth through to the end of the fillet.

To make breadcrumbs, save any dry, slightly stale bread or discarded crusts – or use fresh bread that's been dried (but not toasted) in a low oven – and whizz in a food processor to a fine consistency. Use immediately or store in a resealable freezer bag in the freezer for a ready supply. The breadcrumbs defrost quickly so can be used straight away.

TARRAGON-CRUSTED SEA BASS

Quick and easy to make, this is great for a family meal or for entertaining. The fried breadcrumbs make a deliciously crispy coating while the tarragon sauce is full of tangy flavour and keeps the fish moist. Serve with baby new potatoes and some spinach, samphire or tender-stem broccoli.

SERVES 4

COOK TIME:
12–15 MINUTES

4 sea bass fillets (about 100g/4oz each), skin on (see tip)

40g (1½oz) butter

60g (2½oz) panko breadcrumbs

Finely grated zest of 1 lemon

½ tbsp chopped tarragon

40g (1½oz) Parmesan cheese, coarsely grated

Salt and freshly ground black pepper

4 lemon wedges, to serve

FOR THE LEMON TARRAGON SAUCE

200g (7oz) full-fat crème fraîche

½ tbsp chopped tarragon

1 tbsp lemon juice

A pinch of caster sugar

1. Season the sea bass fillets well on both sides with salt and pepper. Melt the butter in a small pan, then remove from the heat, add the breadcrumbs, lemon zest and tarragon and toss together before setting aside.

2. Lay a sheet of baking paper on a large baking sheet and sprinkle over half the fried breadcrumbs in four rows (each roughly the same size as the fillets). Sit each fillet, skin side down, on top of a row of breadcrumbs and press firmly into the crumbs. Top each fillet with the remaining breadcrumbs and sprinkle with the Parmesan (see tip). Chill in the fridge until 15 minutes before serving.

3. When you are ready to serve, preheat the oven to 200°C/180°C fan/Gas 6.

4. To make the sauce, place the crème fraîche, tarragon, lemon juice and sugar in a bowl. Season with salt and pepper and mix together.

5. Bake the fish in the oven for 12–15 minutes, then carefully lift off with a fish slice and serve with a dollop of the sauce and a wedge of lemon.

PREPARE AHEAD

Prepare completely up to 8 hours ahead and keep in the fridge, then cook to serve.

The sauce can be made up to 2 days ahead and kept in the fridge.

MARY'S EVERYDAY TIPS

This recipe would work equally well with trout fillets or lemon sole. Just be sure to use fillets, as these are thin and flat, rather than steaks, which are chunky.

The breadcrumbs on top of the fish will brown nicely, but sitting the fish, skin side down, on top of the breadcrumbs also gives a lovely crispy base.

SEA BREAM WITH SAMPHIRE AND CHIVES

A delicate-tasting fish, sea bream is similar to sea bass, which would work equally well in this recipe. With its crisp texture and distinctive taste – not unlike asparagus – samphire provides the perfect accompaniment. An elegant dish, it's also incredibly quick to knock up. The recipe serves four, but allow two fillets per person for larger appetites.

SERVES 4

COOK TIME:
10–15 MINUTES

4 sea bream fillets, skin on

1 tbsp sunflower oil

175g (6oz) samphire

1 lemon, cut into
   wedges, to serve

FOR THE SAUCE

150ml (5fl oz) white wine

150ml (5fl oz) pouring
   double cream

2 tbsp snipped chives

Juice of 1 small lemon

Salt and freshly ground
   black pepper

1. First make the sauce. Measure the wine into a small saucepan and boil to reduce by half. Add the cream and boil for a few minutes to thicken the sauce. Add the chives and lemon juice, and season with salt and pepper.

2. Place a large frying pan over a high heat and season the sea bream fillets on both sides with salt and pepper. Add the oil to pan and pan-fry the fish, skin side down, for 2 minutes (see tip). Using a fish slice, carefully turn over the fillets and cook for a further 2 minutes (see tip).

3. Meanwhile, blanche the samphire in boiling water (see tip) for 30 seconds and drain.

4. Divide the samphire between the plates and place a sea bream fillet on top of each. Spoon over the sauce and serve with the lemon wedges.

PREPARE AHEAD

The sauce can be made a day ahead and reheated.

MARY'S EVERYDAY TIPS

The skin on the fish needs to be really crispy, so make sure it is well done on one side before turning over. Don't be tempted to try and turn it before it is ready as it will stick to the pan. When the skin has crisped enough, a fish slice will glide underneath it easily.

There's no need to add any salt to the cooking water as the samphire is naturally salty.

For best results, cook the fish in two batches so they are not crowded in the pan and cook properly.

GOLDEN FRIED CRAB AND BASIL SPAGHETTI

Lovely and light, and using the finest ingredients, this is one of the quickest pasta dishes to make. The flavours of the crab, wine and cream intermingle beautifully, lifted by the lemon and basil. A whole dressed crab consists of both white and brown meat – the brown meat giving richness to the dish – but you can use just white meat if you prefer. Dressed crab in the shell is easily obtainable from a supermarket or fishmonger, or you can buy a pack of mixed crabmeat, or just the white or brown meat on its own. Tins of dressed crab make a good standby otherwise.

SERVES 6

COOK TIME:
25 MINUTES

350g (12oz) dried spaghetti

2 tbsp olive oil

1 onion, finely chopped

1 garlic clove, crushed

100ml (3½fl oz) white wine

150ml (5fl oz) pouring
   double cream

1 dressed crab (about 120g
   in the shell), removed
   from shell and the
   shell discarded

Juice and finely grated
   zest of 1 lemon

100g (4oz) fresh
   white crabmeat

75g (3oz) fresh white
   breadcrumbs

Large bunch of fresh basil,
   chopped, plus extra whole
   leaves to garnish

Salt and freshly ground
   black pepper

1. Cook the spaghetti in a saucepan of boiling salted water according to the packet instructions.

2. While the spaghetti is cooking, heat half the oil in large, deep frying pan (it needs to be large enough to toss the spaghetti into the sauce). Add the onion and cook over a high heat for 3–4 minutes. Lower the heat, cover with a lid and cook for a further 10 minutes or until tender (see tip). Add the garlic and fry over a high heat for a minute.

3. Pour in the wine and boil until reduced by just under half. (This will only take a couple of minutes in a large pan.) Add the cream with the dressed crabmeat, lemon juice and half the lemon zest. Sprinkle in most of the basil (reserving some to garnish), season with salt and pepper and cook, stirring continuously, for a few minutes until combined.

4. Drain the spaghetti and add to the wine and crab sauce, stirring it in to coat well in the sauce.

5. In a separate pan, heat the remaining oil until hot, then add the fresh white crabmeat with the breadcrumbs and the remaining lemon zest and fry for a couple of minutes until golden.

6. Divide the spaghetti between bowls and serve scattered with the fried crabmeat and reserved basil.

MARY'S EVERYDAY TIP

If the onions are cooking too quickly and starting to burn, or if the pan doesn't have a lid, scrunch up a piece of greaseproof or baking paper, wet it so that it doesn't burn and push it into the pan to cover the onions completely. Remove once the onions are tender, increase the heat and add the garlic to finish off.

VEGETARIAN

Fresh and full of flavour, vegetarian meals can be something really special. My Melanzane Pasta (page 180) is a household favourite, and the Potato, Leek and Cheese Pie (page 186) is a hearty meal for the whole family.

SPAGHETTI WITH COURGETTES, TOMATOES AND CHILLI

Light and healthy but full of flavour, this is great for a midweek supper. It's also perfect for using up a glut of courgettes. The sun-blushed tomatoes (see tip) have a lovely intense taste, while the chilli adds a nice hint of heat to the dish.

SERVES 6

COOK TIME: 10 MINUTES

225g (8oz) spaghetti

2 tbsp olive oil

3 large courgettes, cut into 1cm (½in) chunks

1 fresh red chilli, deseeded (optional) and finely chopped

2 large garlic cloves, crushed

200g (7oz) sun-blushed tomatoes in oil, roughly chopped

3 tbsp oil reserved from the tub of tomatoes

1 bunch of parsley, roughly chopped

Juice of ½ lemon

50g (2oz) Parmesan cheese, grated

Salt and freshly ground black pepper

1. Boil the spaghetti in boiling salted water according to the packet instructions or until just cooked. Drain in a colander, reserving 75ml (2½fl oz) of the pasta cooking water.

2. Meanwhile, heat the oil in a large, deep frying pan, add the courgettes, chilli and garlic and fry over a medium–high heat for 3–4 minutes until just softened and browned. Add the sun-blushed tomatoes and the reserved tomato oil.

3. Toss everything together, then add the parsley, cooked pasta and reserved pasta water. Season with salt and pepper and heat through gently, tossing everything together in the pan.

4. Transfer to a warmed serving dish, stir in the lemon juice and sprinkle with the Parmesan.

PREPARE AHEAD

The ingredients can all be prepared ahead, but the dish itself is best made and served immediately.

MARY'S EVERYDAY TIP

Sun-blushed tomatoes – which may also be labelled 'sun-kissed' or 'sun-soaked' – come in oil in a tub (usually found in the chiller cabinet) or jar when you buy them at a supermarket or deli.

FRESH AND SUN-DRIED TOMATO PASTA WITH MOZZARELLA AND BASIL

This is my kind of food – quick to make and full of sun-kissed Mediterranean flavours! Buy deep red tomatoes as they have the best flavour and strength. If the skins are very thick, you may wish to skin them (see tip on page 176), but that might be a bit a bit too much to do for an everyday kitchen supper.

SERVES 6

COOK TIME: 10 MINUTES

350g (12oz) penne pasta

4 tbsp olive oil

4 garlic cloves, crushed

1 fresh red chilli, deseeded and finely chopped

100g (4oz) sun-dried tomatoes (see tip), chopped

3 tbsp sun-dried tomato paste

900g (2lb) just-ripe, thin-skinned red tomatoes (see tip on page 176), chopped

Juice of 1 lemon

1 bunch of basil, chopped

30g (1oz) Parmesan cheese, grated

1 mozzarella ball (about 150g/5oz drained weight), drained and torn into pieces

Salt and freshly ground black pepper

1. Cook the penne in boiling salted water according to the packet instructions. Drain in a colander, reserving 100ml (3½fl oz) of the pasta cooking water.

2. Meanwhile, heat the oil in a frying pan, add the garlic and chilli and fry over a high heat for 1 minute, stirring. Add the sun-dried tomatoes and paste, followed by the fresh tomatoes and reserved pasta water. Stir together, then raise the heat and boil for a couple of minutes until the tomatoes start to break down and release their juices.

3. Add the lemon juice, cooked pasta and two-thirds of the basil, season with salt and pepper and toss together for about 2 minutes. Add the Parmesan and tip into a warmed serving dish. Scatter with the mozzarella and remaining basil to serve.

MARY'S EVERYDAY TIP

Sun-dried tomatoes are available dried or in oil – either would be suitable for use here. If you have time, it's best to soak the dried ones according to the packet instructions as they contain salt as part of the drying/preserving process. The ones in oil need to be drained. first, but the oil could be used for frying, in place of the olive oil, to give maximum flavour. They differ from sun-blushed tomatoes (see Spaghetti with Courgettes, Tomatoes and Chilli on page 170), which are not fully dried and therefore have a shorter shelf life.

Tomatoes should be stored at room temperature for the best flavour; they will continue to ripen if kept on a windowsill.

ROMANO PEPPERS WITH HERBS AND LEMON DRESSING

Here Romano peppers are roasted just enough to soften them and give a delicious sweet roasted flavour while retaining some bite and holding their shape. The rich herby cheese filling is lifted by the taste of lemon, both in the filling and the dressing. Serve warm as a starter or cold as a side dish or to include on a buffet table. If you're making these as a starter – serving one half per person – try to buy peppers that aren't too long so that they fit neatly on each plate.

SERVES 6 AS A STARTER OR SIDE DISH

COOK TIME: 20 MINUTES

3 red Romano peppers

1 tbsp olive oil

Salt and freshly ground black pepper

100g (4oz) rocket leaves, to serve

FOR THE HERB FILLING

1 x 280g tub of full-fat cream cheese (see tip)

25g (1oz) chopped basil

3 tbsp finely snipped chives

3 tbsp chopped parsley

Finely grated zest of ½ lemon

1 tbsp lemon juice

25g (1oz) Parmesan cheese, grated

FOR THE LEMON DRESSING

Finely grated zest of ½ lemon

90ml (3fl oz) good olive oil

2 tbsp lemon juice

2 tsp caster sugar

1 tsp Dijon mustard

1. Preheat the oven to 200°C/180°C fan/Gas 6.

2. Slice each pepper in half lengthways, through the stem. Remove the seeds and any white membrane.

3. Sit the peppers, cut side up, on a baking sheet, season each half with salt and pepper and drizzle with the tablespoon of olive oil. Roast in the oven for 10 minutes, then remove and leave to cool slightly.

4. Meanwhile, place the filling ingredients in a bowl, season well with salt and pepper and mix to combine. Divide the mixture evenly between the pepper halves, spreading it out to fill each pepper right to each end. Return to the oven for a further 10 minutes until the peppers are tender.

5. Measure the dressing ingredients into a jug or bowl, season with salt and pepper and whisk well to combine.

6. Serve the hot peppers, one half per person, on a bed of rocket, drizzled with the lemon dressing.

PREPARE AHEAD

The peppers can be cooked up to 8 hours ahead and served cold.

The filling can be made up to a day ahead and kept in the fridge.

The dressing can be made ahead and stored in the fridge, in a jar with a lid, for 2–3 days.

MARY'S EVERYDAY TIP

You need to use full-fat cream cheese for the filling. If low-fat is used, the mixture will be too runny and slide off the peppers.

PLUM TOMATO, OLIVE AND MARJORAM TART

I make this in a long, thin tranche tin – just as I do for the Apple and Lemon Galette on page 240. It gives a lovely shape, but if you don't have a tranche tin, a 23cm (9in) round flan tin would make a good alternative. Marjoram is a herb I often grow in my garden but don't use that much as I tend to go for my favourites of basil, parsley, dill, chives or mint. However, it works really well with the tomato and olive combination here. If the fresh herb is hard to come by, you can use a mixture of fresh thyme and basil.

SERVES 6

COOK TIME:
45–50 MINUTES

FOR THE PASTRY

150g (5oz) plain flour, plus extra for dusting

75g (3oz) butter, chilled and cut into cubes

1 egg, beaten

FOR THE FILLING

2 eggs

200ml (7fl oz) full-fat crème fraîche

50g (2oz) Cheddar cheese, grated

50g (2oz) Parmesan cheese, grated

1 tbsp finely chopped marjoram

6 large plum tomatoes, skinned (see tip) and sliced into rounds

12 pitted black olives, halved

½ tbsp balsamic vinegar

Salt and freshly ground black pepper

1. You will need a 12 x 36cm (5 x 14in) loose-bottomed tranche tin with 2.5–3cm (1–1¼in) sides.

2. First make the pastry. Measure the flour and butter into a food processor and whizz until the mixture is like breadcrumbs. Alternatively, place the dry ingredients in a mixing bowl and rub in the butter with your fingertips. Add the egg and whizz again until a ball of dough is formed.

3. Sprinkle your work surface with flour and roll out the dough until it is the thickness of a £1 coin and large enough to fit the tin (see tips). Line the base and sides with the pastry, leaving a generous edge to allow for shrinkage in the oven, prick the pastry all over with a fork and chill in the fridge for 30 minutes.

4. Meanwhile, preheat the oven to 200°C/180°C fan/Gas 6 and place a large baking sheet inside to get very hot.

5. To make the filling, break the eggs into a jug or bowl, add the crème fraîche, both cheeses and half the marjoram. Season with salt and pepper and mix until combined.

6. Line the pastry case with baking paper and baking beans, place it on the hot baking sheet and bake blind for 15 minutes (see tip on page 240). Remove the paper and beans and return to the oven for a further 5 minutes to dry out.

7. Remove the pastry case from the oven and lower the oven temperature to 180°C/160°C fan/Gas 4.

8. Pour the filling into the pastry case and lay the tomato slices overlapping in five or six rows widthways across the top. Arrange the olive halves in

Recipe continues overleaf

between the rows of tomatoes and sprinkle with the remaining marjoram. Brush the tomatoes and olives with the balsamic vinegar.

9. Bake in the oven for 25–30 minutes until the pastry is golden and cooked and the top is browned. Trim the edges to remove any overhanging pastry, then carefully remove from the tin and serve warm with dressed salad leaves.

PREPARE AHEAD

Can be made up to a day ahead and reheated to serve.

MARY'S EVERYDAY TIPS

To skin tomatoes, cut a cross in the top of each tomato, place in a bowl and cover with boiling water. Leave to stand for a couple of minutes, then drain and rinse in cold water. The skins will now peel off easily.

The trick with pastry is to ensure everything is as cold as possible. On a warm day, it's best to allow the pastry to rest for 15 minutes before lining the tin.

A good tip for making rolled-out pastry easier to transfer to a tart tin is to roll it out on the removable base of the tin. Roll out the pastry larger than the base (so that it covers the sides of the tin), fold the sides in to the middle, then put the base back into the tin. Lift up the sides of the pastry and press into the sides of the tin. Patch any holes with excess pastry and smooth over to ensure the filling can't leak out.

SQUASH AND BLACK BEAN CHILLI

This is very similar to a meat chilli but using tender cubes of butternut squash and black beans, which are readily available in cans. Use canned black eyed beans if not. Serve with boiled rice, guacamole (see page 50), soured cream and grated cheese, or with tortillas, or as a filling for burritos.

SERVES 6–8

COOK TIME: 1 HOUR

1 small butternut squash (about 1kg/1lb 12oz), peeled, deseeded and cut into cubes

3 tbsp olive oil

2 red onions, chopped

2 garlic cloves, crushed

1 fresh red chilli, deseeded and finely chopped

1 tbsp ground cumin

1 tbsp ground coriander

3 x 400g tins of chopped tomatoes

150ml (5fl oz) white wine

1 tbsp light muscovado sugar

2 x 400g tins of black beans (see tip), drained and rinsed

Salt and freshly ground black pepper

sprigs of coriander, to serve

1. Preheat the oven for 220°C/200°C fan/Gas 7.

2. Arrange the cubes of squash in a single layer a baking tray and drizzle over 2 tablespoons of the olive oil. Season with salt and pepper and toss together. Roast in the oven for 25–35 minutes or until golden and tender but still with a little bite.

3. Heat the remaining oil in a large, wide deep frying pan. Add the onions, garlic and chilli and fry over a high heat for 2–3 minutes. Sprinkle in the spices and fry for another minute. Add the tomatoes (see tip), wine and sugar, season with salt and pepper and bring to the boil, stirring. Cover with a lid, then reduce the heat and simmer for about 10 minutes.

4. Give the mixture a stir, add the beans and the roasted cubes of squash, then cover again with the lid and simmer for a further 10 minutes.

5. Check the seasoning and serve piping hot with the coriander.

PREPARE AHEAD

Can be made up to a day ahead and reheated.

FREEZE *Freezes well.*

MARY'S EVERYDAY TIPS

Black beans are readily available, but you could use kidney beans if you prefer.

Rinse the tins of tomatoes with a little of the wine (or a drop of water) before adding to the pan. This helps clean the tins and means there is no waste!

MELANZANE PASTA

*Layers of lasagne, aubergine (**melanzane** in Italian) and savoury béchamel and tomato and basil sauce, this must be one of my favourite dishes for preparing ahead. Delicious served on its own or with chunks of garlic bread.*

SERVES 6

COOK TIME:
1 HOUR– 1 HOUR
10 MINUTES, PLUS
STANDING

2 large or 3 medium
   aubergines, sliced into
   5mm (¼in) rounds

4 tbsp olive oil, plus extra
   for greasing

5–7 sheets of dried lasagne

Salt and freshly ground
   black pepper

FOR THE
BÉCHAMEL SAUCE

50g (2oz) butter

50g (2oz) plain flour

600ml (1 pint) milk

1 tsp Dijon mustard

100g (4oz) Parmesan
   cheese, grated

FOR THE
TOMATO SAUCE

2 garlic cloves, crushed

1 x 400g tin of chopped
   tomatoes

500ml (18fl oz)
   tomato passata

1 bunch of basil, chopped

2 tsp caster sugar

1. You will need a 2-litre (3½-pint) wide-based ovenproof dish (see tip). Preheat the oven to 200°C/180°C fan/Gas 6, then grease the dish with oil and line two baking sheets with baking paper.

2. Arrange the aubergine slices in a single layer on the prepared baking sheets. Drizzle over the oil and season with salt and pepper. Roast in the oven for 20–25 minutes, turning over the slices halfway through the cooking time. Remove from the oven and set aside.

3. Meanwhile, lay the pasta sheets in a dish, cover with boiling water and leave to soften for 10 minutes.

4. To make the béchamel sauce, melt the butter in a saucepan over a gentle heat, sprinkle in the flour and whisk for 2–3 minutes over a high heat until smooth. Heat the milk in a separate pan, then gradually blend into the butter and flour roux. Bring to the boil and allow to bubble for about 5 minutes, whisking the sauce until smooth (see tip).

5. Add the mustard and two-thirds of the cheese, season with salt and pepper and stir until the cheese has melted. Keep warm over a very low heat while you prepare the rest of the dish.

6. Place all the ingredients for the tomato sauce in a large bowl, season well with salt and pepper and mix together. Drain the pasta and separate the sheets.

7. To assemble the dish, spread a third of the tomato sauce in the base of the dish, then a third of the béchamel sauce. Arrange a third of the aubergines on top in a single layer, followed by half the sheets of lasagne (see tip). Repeat the process, so that you have three layers of aubergine/sauces and two layers of pasta (aubergine will be the top layer), then sprinkle with the rest of the Parmesan.

Recipe continues overleaf

8. Leave to stand for a minimum of 1 hour (or store overnight in the fridge) before cooking.

9. Bake in the oven for 40–45 minutes until bubbling and golden on top. Leave to stand for 5 minutes before serving.

PREPARE AHEAD

Can be assembled up to a day ahead, then stored in the fridge and cooked to serve.

Leftovers keep well for up to 3 days.

MARY'S EVERYDAY TIPS

It is important to use the right-sized dish so that the layers are all the correct thickness and the dish cooks evenly.

The key to a good béchamel sauce is to keep stirring! If the hot milk starts to bubble too much when it is being added to the roux, then turn down the heat a little, to give yourself more time to stir it in and incorporate it.

During assembly, you may need to break the lasagne sheets into pieces to make them fit in an even layer. Try not to overlap the sheets or they will not cook evenly. When adding the sauce, make sure the edges of the pasta are well covered with sauce, and not curling up. If they stick up out of the sauce, they will burn during cooking.

AUBERGINE AND TALEGGIO BAKE

Taleggio is a wonderful strong semi-soft cheese that becomes stringy when melted. It's not quite as stringy as mozzarella, although that would make a good alternative here, but has a more distinctive flavour and is available in most supermarkets these days. The cheese melts to give a sauce-like effect within the aubergine rolls, while the onion adds sweetness and the tomato sauce gives a lovely sharp contrast. Great as a side dish and hearty enough to serve on its own.

SERVES 4 AS A MAIN AND 8 AS A SIDE DISH

COOK TIME:
40 MINUTES

2 medium aubergines

3 tbsp olive oil

2 onions, thinly sliced (see tip)

1 tsp muscovado sugar

1 tsp balsamic vinegar

200g (7oz) Taleggio cheese, cut into 16 cubes

300ml (10fl oz) passata

1 garlic clove, crushed

25g (1oz) Parmesan cheese, finely grated

Salt and freshly ground black pepper

1. You will need a 1.75-litre (3-pint) wide-based, shallow ovenproof dish. Preheat the oven to 200°C/180°C fan/Gas 6 and line two baking sheets with baking paper.

2. Slice each aubergine lengthways into 5mm (¼in) slices – you should get about eight slices out of each one. Brush the slices on each side with some of the oil and season with salt and pepper. Arrange in a single layer on the prepared baking sheets. Roast in the oven for about 15 minutes or until just soft and lightly golden, then set aside to cool on the baking sheets.

3. Meanwhile, heat the remaining oil in a frying pan, and fry the onions for 3–4 minutes over a high heat. Cover with a lid, lower the heat and gently fry for about 15 minutes until soft, stirring occasionally. Remove the lid and increase the heat, then add the sugar and vinegar and fry over a high heat for a couple of minutes until lightly golden and the liquid has evaporated.

4. Top the cooled aubergines (still on the baking sheets) with the onion mixture (see tip), dividing it evenly between the slices – about 1 teaspoon per slice. Put one cube of cheese on one end of each slice and then roll up like a cigar to encase the cheese.

5. Place the passata and garlic in a jug and season with salt and pepper before pouring into the ovenproof dish. Sit the aubergine rolls on their ends on top of the tomato sauce. Stand the rolls close to each other in rows of four to help them stay rolled up. Sprinkle grated Parmesan all over the top of the rolls and tomato sauce.

6. Bake in the oven for about 20 minutes until piping hot and the cheese has melted. Serve with crusty bread.

PREPARE AHEAD

Can be assembled up to 4 hours ahead.

MARY'S EVERYDAY TIP

For an even quicker dish, onion marmalade or caramelised onion chutney could be used to spread on the aubergine slices instead of the onion, sugar and vinegar mixture.

ORZO WITH BROAD BEANS, PEAS, LEMON AND THYME

Orzo is a type of pasta made in the shape of a large grain of rice. It's a bit different yet very versatile – I find I use it more and more. It can be served on its own or used in a range of dishes, from soups and salads to casseroles. The recipe I've included here is rather like a risotto. Orzo grains remain more separate than risotto rice, but the finished dish is just as creamy and tasty. It's also much quicker to prepare, making it perfect for an everyday lunch or supper.

SERVES 4

COOK TIME:
15–20 MINUTES

200g (7oz) dried orzo

200g (7oz) frozen baby broad beans, defrosted and outer skin removed

200g (7oz) frozen petits pois, defrosted

A knob of butter

1 tbsp oil

1 onion, very thinly sliced

2 garlic cloves, crushed

200g (7oz) full-fat crème fraîche

1 tbsp chopped thyme leaves

Juice and finely grated zest of 1 lemon

25g (1oz) Parmesan cheese, coarsely grated

Salt and freshly ground black pepper

TO SERVE

25g (1oz) pine nuts, toasted (see tip)

25g (1oz) Parmesan cheese, coarsely grated

1. Cook the orzo in boiling salted water according to the packet instructions (usually about 10 minutes) or until just cooked (see tip), then drain. Boil the broad beans and petits pois in a separate pan for 2–3 minutes, then drain and rinse.

2. Meanwhile, heat the butter and oil in a large frying pan, and when the butter has melted, add the onion and fry over a high heat for 2–3 minutes. Cover with a lid, then reduce the heat and cook gently for about 15 minutes or until soft. Add the garlic, turn up the heat and fry for 1 minute.

3. Stir in the crème fraîche, then add the cooked orzo, beans and peas and gently heat together. Add the thyme, lemon juice and zest and Parmesan, stir together and season to taste with salt and pepper.

4. Spoon into a serving dish and scatter with the pine nuts and grated Parmesan to serve.

MARY'S EVERYDAY TIPS

Don't overcook the pasta as it will absorb the cream on standing and it shouldn't be too stodgy.

Toast the pine nuts in a dry pan over a medium heat for 4–5 minutes, tossing frequently to ensure they don't burn. You could use ready-toasted pine nuts otherwise.

POTATO, LEEK AND CHEESE PIE

Crisp layered pastry over a gorgeous creamy filling, this is pure comfort food – great for feeding the whole family. Flaky pastry is like puff pastry but not as rich. Using a mixture of lard and butter, rather than all butter, adds to the texture.

SERVES 6–8

COOK TIME:
1 HOUR – 1 HOUR
10 MINUTES,
PLUS CHILLING

**FOR THE FAST
FLAKY PASTRY**

125g (4½oz) butter

125g (4½oz) lard

350g (12oz) plain flour,
  plus extra for dusting

1 egg, beaten, for brushing

FOR THE PIE FILLING

60g (2½oz) butter

2 small leeks (about 150g/5oz
  each), thinly sliced

1 onion, thinly sliced

450g (1lb) potatoes (about
  2 medium), peeled and cut
  into 2cm (¾in) cubes

600ml (1 pint) milk

50g (2oz) plain flour

1 tbsp Dijon mustard

1 tbsp chopped thyme leaves

50g (2oz) mature Cheddar
  cheese, grated

50g (2oz) Parmesan
  cheese, grated

Salt and freshly
  ground black pepper

1. You will need a 25cm (10in) round pie dish.

2. Leave the butter and lard for the pastry in the freezer for 1 hour.

3. To make the pie filling, melt the butter in a wide-based saucepan or deep frying pan, add the leeks and onion and fry over a high heat for 2–3 minutes. Cover with a lid, then lower the heat and cook for 10–15 minutes or until tender but not browned.

4. Meanwhile, boil the potatoes in salted water in a separate pan for 8–10 minutes until just tender. Drain well. Heat the milk in a separate pan until just coming to the boil and remove from the heat.

5. Remove the lid from the pan with the leeks and onion, turn up the heat to drive off any excess liquid, then sprinkle in the flour. Stir in and cook for 1 minute, then gradually blend in the hot milk and bring to the boil, stirring. Leave to bubble for about 5 minutes until thickened, then add the mustard, thyme and the two cheeses and season to taste with salt and pepper.

6. Add the cooked potatoes to the sauce and stir in. Pour the filling into the pie dish and sit a pie funnel (or an upturned eggcup) in the middle of the dish to support the pastry. Cover and set aside until the filling is stone cold (see tip).

7. To make the pastry, measure the flour into a large bowl. Take the butter and lard straight from the freezer and coarsely grate into the flour (see tip). Add 150ml (5fl oz) of water and stir together to combine into a firm dough.

8. Sprinkle a work surface with flour, add the dough and knead until smooth. Roll into a rectangle about 20 x 50cm (8 x 20in), then fold up the bottom third of the pastry to the middle and fold the top third down over it, creating three layers. Turn the pastry through 90 degrees, roll again and fold, then turn and fold twice again to give 12 layers in total. Wrap in cling film and chill in the fridge for a minimum of 30 minutes.

Recipe continues overleaf

9. Meanwhile, preheat the oven to 220°C/200°C fan/Gas 7.

10. Roll the pastry on a floured work surface until about as thick as a £1 coin and cut out a disc 3cm (1¼in) bigger than the pie dish. Cut a long thin strip about 1cm (½in) wide to fit around the top of the dish. Wet the lip of the dish, lay the thin strip of pastry on top and press down (see tip). Wet the top of the pastry lip and lay the pastry disc on top, pressing down and crimping the edge.

11. Re-roll the pastry trimmings and cut out leaf shapes for decoration (see tip). Brush the top with some of the beaten egg and arrange the leaves on top. Make a little hole in the centre. Brush the top of the pie with more beaten egg and sit it on a baking sheet.

12. Bake in the oven for 40–45 minutes or until crisp and golden on top and the filling is piping hot. Serve with a green vegetable.

PREPARE AHEAD

The base can be made and left in the pie dish up to a day ahead. Top with the pastry up to 6 hours before cooking.

The pastry can be prepared ahead and chilled in the fridge overnight.

FREEZE *Both the pastry and the pie freeze well uncooked.*

MARY'S EVERYDAY TIPS

Wrap the butter and lard blocks in kitchen paper and use this to hold the fat while grating.

The filling needs to cool down completely as any residual heat will start melting the pastry and cause it to sink when baking in the oven.

Adding a strip of pastry to the edge of the pie dish helps raise the pastry a little and prevents it from going soggy during cooking.

Don't re-knead the trimmings – lay them on top of each other and then roll, as this keeps the layers in the pastry intact.

PORTOBELLO MUSHROOMS WITH DOUBLE CHEESE TOPPING

Portobello mushrooms are large and open, firm on top with woody gills underneath. They are so versatile – delicious with this creamy, cheesy filling with a sprinkling of paprika for added flavour and a dash of colour. This dish would be perfect for supper with a salad, or as a starter if entertaining. You could also serve it as a side dish for a barbecue or buffet.

SERVES 4–6

COOK TIME:
15 MINUTES

6 large Portobello
 mushrooms

25g (1oz) butter, softened

FOR THE FILLING

180g (7oz) full-fat
 cream cheese

75g (3oz) mature Cheddar
 cheese, grated

2 garlic cloves, crushed

4 tomatoes, deseeded
 and diced

2 tbsp snipped chives

Paprika, for sprinkling

Salt and freshly ground
 black pepper

1. Preheat the oven to 200°C/180°C fan/Gas 6 and line a baking sheet with baking paper.

2. Carefully peel the skins from the mushrooms and remove the stalks if chunky (see tip). Spread the peeled top of each mushroom with butter and place, buttered side down, on the prepared baking sheet.

3. Add the cream cheese and 50g (2oz) of the Cheddar to a bowl with the garlic, tomatoes and chives, mix together and season with salt and pepper. Spoon the filling on to the gill side of each mushroom, spreading it evenly. Top with the remaining Cheddar and sprinkle with paprika.

4. Bake in the oven for about 15 minutes or until bubbling and golden (see tip). Serve hot with dressed rocket leaves and crusty bread.

PREPARE AHEAD

Can be assembled ready for the oven and kept in the fridge up to 8 hours ahead.

MARY'S EVERYDAY TIPS

You can chop up the stalks and add them to the filling, if you prefer, rather than throwing them away.

Portobello mushrooms have a great flavour, but be careful not to overcook them or too much liquid may be released and the flavour will be lost.

SIDES AND
SALADS

A delicious side dish or salad is always a welcome addition to dinner. A creamy Tartiflette (page 205) or a lighter Fennel and Watermelon Salad (page 214) will enhance the main dish, and add colour and interest to the table.

CELERIAC AND LEEK GRATIN

Creamy and delicious, this is a bit different from the standard gratin dauphinois. Celeriac has a more distinctive flavour than potato, which gives this dish more character. It is just as tender, though, with a slight bite and additional texture from the chunky pieces of soft leek.

SERVES 6

**COOK TIME:
1 HOUR, PLUS
STANDING**

Butter or oil, for greasing

3 leeks, cut into 2cm (¾in) slices

500g (1lb 2oz) celeriac (about 1 small)

300ml (10fl oz) pouring double cream

300ml (10fl oz) milk

100g (4oz) Gruyère cheese, grated

50g (2oz) coarse fresh white breadcrumbs

About ½ tsp paprika

Salt and freshly ground black pepper

1. You will need a 2-litre (3½-pint) wide-based ovenproof dish. Preheat the oven to 200°C/180°C fan/Gas 6 and grease the dish with a little butter or oil.

2. Cook the leek slices in boiling salted water for 5 minutes or until just soft. Drain well and dry on kitchen paper.

3. Peel the celeriac with a sharp knife and then cut into ultra-thin slices (see tip). Arrange half over the base of the prepared dish. Mix the cream and milk together in a jug and season with salt and pepper. Pour half over the celeriac and then scatter with half the grated cheese. Arrange the cooked leeks on top, followed by the remaining celeriac in an even layer. Pour over the remaining cream mixture and season again with salt and pepper.

4. Cover the dish with foil and bake in the oven for 35 minutes. Remove the foil and sprinkle with the remaining cheese, the breadcrumbs and paprika. Return to the oven (without the foil) and cook for further 20 minutes until bubbling and golden on top and the celeriac is tender.

5. Leave to stand for 5 minutes before serving.

PREPARE AHEAD

Can be cooked up to 8 hours ahead and reheated in a hot oven to serve (see also tip).

MARY'S EVERYDAY TIPS

If you want to make the dish ahead, but not cook it, blanch the celeriac slices in boiling water for about 3 minutes with the leeks. Cooking the celeriac a little will prevent the slices from going brown.

Use a mandolin or the fine cutter of a food processor to speed up the slicing process for thin uniform slices of celeriac. This cuts down the preparation time significantly.

GREEN VEGETABLE STIR-FRY

So quick and easy for supper, whether as a side dish or tossed with noodles as a main. The vegetables are very lightly cooked so they stay crunchy and vivid green. A tender-leaved cabbage, savoy is perfect for this recipe, as is pointed cabbage. The soy seasons the stir-fried vegetables, so no additional salt may be needed.

SERVES 4–6

COOK TIME:
6–8 MINUTES

2 tbsp olive oil

A knob of butter

1 fennel bulb, trimmed, core removed and bulb thinly sliced

2 large courgettes, halved lengthways and cut into 1cm (½in) slices

1 small savoy cabbage, tough core removed and leaves very finely sliced (see tip)

Juice of ½ lemon

1 tbsp dark soy sauce

Salt and freshly ground black pepper

2 tbsp chopped parsley, to garnish

1. Heat the oil and butter in a large frying pan or wok over a high heat. When the butter has melted, add the fennel and courgettes and stir-fry over a high heat for 2–3 minutes or until tinged brown and starting to soften.

2. Tip in the cabbage and stir-fry for another 2–3 minutes. Add the lemon juice and soy sauce. Season with pepper and a little salt to taste (you may not need it), then toss until heated through.

3. Serve piping hot and sprinkled with the parsley.

PREPARE AHEAD

The vegetables can be sliced in advance, up to 6 hours ahead, ready to cook later in the day.

MARY'S EVERYDAY TIP

To prepare the cabbage, remove the outer dark green leaves and cut out the tough core, then roll the leaves up tightly and cut into strips. Slice the remaining heart in half and cut into strips.

SWEDE PURÉE

Such a favourite of mine and my family – great to make ahead too. The same recipe would work well with a mixture of celeriac and potato. Add a little nutmeg, if you like.

SERVES 6

COOK TIME:
20–25 MINUTES

1.4kg (3lb) swedes,
  peeled and cut into
  2cm (¾in) chunks

50g (2oz) butter

Salt and freshly ground
  black pepper

1. Bring a large pan of salted water to the boil, add the chunks of swede and boil for 20–25 minutes or until tender.

2. Drain, allow the swede to cool slightly and then transfer to a food processor (see tip). Add the butter, season with salt and pepper and whizz for a minute until smooth. Do this in batches for the best results. Serve hot.

PREPARE AHEAD

Can be made up to 3 hours ahead. Once puréed, spoon into a buttered ovenproof dish and leave to cool, then reheat in a hot oven to serve.

MARY'S EVERYDAY TIP

Alternatively, use a potato masher or mouli grater for a smooth finish.

CELERIAC AND TARRAGON REMOULADE

I adore celeriac remoulade – so much lovelier than coleslaw. And it's so simple to make too – the celeriac softens in the mayonnaise dressing and the flavours develop and complement each other well.

SERVES 6–8

PREP TIME:
20 MINUTES,
PLUS CHILLING

1 small celeriac (about
600g/1lb 5oz)

FOR THE DRESSING

200g (7oz) full-fat
mayonnaise

Juice of 1 small lemon

2 tbsp chopped tarragon

1/2 tsp sugar

Salt and freshly ground
black pepper

1. First make the dressing. Place the mayonnaise, lemon juice, tarragon and sugar in a bowl. Season with salt and pepper and mix together.

2. Using a sharp knife (see tip), peel and slice the celeriac into very thin batons, like matchsticks. Or for speed, use the grater attachment on a food processor to give long strips, or use a spiraliser.

3. Add the celeriac to the mayonnaise and tarragon dressing and toss together.

4. Leave in the fridge for 2–3 hours to soften.

PREPARE AHEAD

Can be made up to 8 hours ahead and stored in the fridge.

MARY'S EVERYDAY TIP

Celeriac is very knobbly and so it's easier to peel the skin with a knife rather than a potato peeler. It also discolours quickly, hence it's best to make the dressing first before cutting the celeriac so that it can be mixed quickly with the dressing. Alternatively, put the celeriac in water with a squeeze of lemon juice or white wine vinegar to stop it discolouring.

GREEN BEANS AND MANGETOUT WITH MINT CAPER BUTTER

This dish would be delicious with lamb or any roast, the mint caper butter giving a twist to the more usual accompaniment of mint sauce. It's one that needs to be served straight away, however, as the vegetables and mint will discolour if kept warm.

SERVES 6

COOK TIME:
5 MINUTES

300g (11oz) fine green beans, trimmed and halved

200g (7oz) baby broad beans (see tip)

200g (7oz) mangetout, halved diagonally

1 tbsp chopped mint

Coarse sea salt and freshly ground black pepper

FOR THE MINT CAPER BUTTER

40g (1½oz) butter

3 tbsp coarsely chopped capers

1 tbsp chopped mint

1. Cook the beans and broad beans in a large saucepan of boiling salted water for 3 minutes. Add the mangetout and cook for a further 2 minutes. Drain and tip into a warmed serving bowl. Add the mint, season with salt and pepper and toss together.

2. To make the mint caper butter, melt the butter in the saucepan (no need to clean it first) over a high heat, then add the capers and mint, and toss to combine.

3. Pour the warm butter over the beans and serve piping hot.

MARY'S EVERYDAY TIP

Baby broad beans are much softer than older ones and may not need popping from their skins. If your beans are older, however, it may be best to remove the skins first: cook separately before removing the skins and then toss in butter with the other cooked vegetables.

TARTIFLETTE

Rich and very moreish, tartiflette comes from the Savoy region in the French Alps. I've included Camembert, for a slight twist to the classic recipe, but you could of course use the more traditional reblochon cheese instead. Waxy potatoes such as Nadine, Estima, Charlotte or Cara give a lovely texture to the dish, much better than using floury potatoes, which could break up when cooking as they are more delicate. Serve on its own or with a mixed grill.

SERVES 6 AS A SIDE AND 4 AS A MAIN DISH

COOK TIME:
50–55 MINUTES

1kg (2lb 3oz) waxy potatoes, peeled and sliced into 5mm (½in) discs (see tip)

1 tbsp oil

200g (7oz) rashers of smoked bacon (see tip), cut into thin strips

2 onions, finely sliced

1 x 250g (9oz) Camembert cheese, sliced into 1cm (½in) strips (see tip)

125ml (4fl oz) white wine

125ml (4fl oz) double cream

Salt and freshly ground black pepper

1. You will need a 1.75-litre (3-pint) wide-based ovenproof dish. Preheat the oven to 200°C/180°C fan/Gas 6.

2. Put the potato slices into a deep saucepan, cover with cold water and season with salt. Bring to the boil and cook for about 10 minutes or until just tender. Drain and allow to cool.

3. Heat the oil in a frying pan, add the bacon and fry for 3–5 minutes until crisp and golden. Remove with a slotted spoon and set aside. Add the onions and fry for a minute, then cover the pan with a lid, lower the heat and cook for 15 minutes until soft. Remove from the pan and set aside with the bacon.

4. Take the ovenproof dish and arrange the potatoes in even layers, sprinkling each layer with some of the onions, bacon and cheese. Season with salt and pepper in between each layer and finish with slices of cheese on top. Mix the wine and cream together in a bowl and pour over the potatoes.

5. Bake in the oven for 20–25 minutes until bubbling and lightly golden.

PREPARE AHEAD

Can be assembled up to 4 hours ahead.

MARY'S EVERYDAY TIPS

For speed, use a food processor to slice the potatoes.

Use good-quality bacon or it will release water rather than fat, which means there is nothing left in the pan to fry the onions.

A 10cm (4in) diameter Camembert will give ten strips. To give more pieces for layering and enough left for the top, cut the longer pieces in half.

BROCCOLI AND CAULIFLOWER STIR-FRY

Making a change from boiled vegetables, this is quick to do and very tasty. Cooked like this, the broccoli and cauliflower retain a nice crunch too. If you like a bit of heat, add plenty of black pepper to the vegetables, or even some chilli flakes.

SERVES 6

COOK TIME:
10–12 MINUTES

1 small cauliflower

1 small head of broccoli

2 tbsp olive oil

2 banana shallots,
  finely sliced

2 garlic cloves, crushed

2 tbsp runny honey

Salt and freshly ground
  black pepper

1. Cut the cauliflower and broccoli into the smallest florets possible – roughly 2cm (¾in) in length. In total, you need about 350g (12oz) of cauliflower florets and 250g (9oz) of broccoli florets; discard any leaves and leftover pieces of stalk (see tip).

2. Heat the oil in a large, wide frying pan or wok until very hot. Add the shallots and stir-fry over a high heat for 2–3 minutes. Add the florets and garlic and stir-fry for another 2–3 minutes or until starting to brown (see tip).

3. Cover with a lid to create a little steam, lower the heat and cook for a further 3 minutes. Remove the lid and fry over a high heat for another couple of minutes until starting to soften but still with a bit of crunch.

4. Season with salt and pepper, pour over the honey and serve.

PREPARE AHEAD

The vegetables can be prepared up to 6 hours ahead for cooking later in the day.

MARY'S EVERYDAY TIPS

Save the leftover stalks and leaves to make soup or stock.

Use two wooden spoons or spatulas, one in each hand, to help toss the vegetables and cook them evenly in the pan.

POTATO SALAD WITH CELERY AND APPLE

This is an old favourite of mine – rather like a cross between potato and Waldorf salad without the nuts! The vinaigrette dressing lightens the mayonnaise, so that the potatoes are soft and creamy, rather than cloyingly stodgy, with added crunch from the apples and celery. You could use other types of new potatoes instead of Jersey Royals. They are the king of new potatoes, but their season is fairly short. Try Charlotte, Nicola or Maris Piper – sometimes they are sold as salad potatoes.

SERVES 6–8

COOK TIME:
15 MINUTES, PLUS
COOLING

1kg (2lb 3oz) Jersey Royal
    or baby new potatoes
    (unpeeled), halved

2 small shallots, thinly sliced

1 red eating apple

Juice of ½ lemon

3 celery sticks, thinly sliced

6–8 tbsp full-fat mayonnaise

Salt and freshly ground
    black pepper

2 tbsp snipped chives,
    to garnish

FOR THE DRESSING

1½ tbsp Dijon mustard

3 tbsp white wine vinegar

5 tbsp good olive oil

1/2 tsp sugar

1. Cook the potatoes in boiling salted water for about 15 minutes or until tender.

2. While the potatoes are cooking, measure the dressing ingredients into a bowl and whisk to combine, seasoning with salt and pepper. Stir in the shallots.

3. Core the apple, leaving it unpeeled, and cut into very small cubes before mixing with the lemon juice in a separate bowl.

4. Drain the potatoes and, while they're still hot, tip into the dressing (see tip). Carefully mix together with a spatula to stop the potatoes breaking up and leave to cool for 10 minutes. Add the apple and celery and season with salt and pepper.

5. Add the mayonnaise to the potato mixture and stir until coated. Spoon into a serving dish and sprinkle with the chives.

PREPARE AHEAD

Can be made up to a day ahead. Store in the fridge and bring up to room temperature to serve.

MARY'S EVERYDAY TIP

Adding the potatoes to the dressing while they are still hot is important, as the potatoes soak up the liquid more easily and absorb the flavour.

RAW PICKLED FENNEL, CUCUMBER AND CORIANDER SALAD

This is fresh and healthy, with lots of colour. Presentation is important, so cut the vegetables attractively and serve on a decorative platter.

SERVES 6

PREP TIME:
15 MINUTES, PLUS MARINATING

25g (1oz) light muscovado sugar

50ml (2fl oz) white wine vinegar

1 fennel bulb

1 small cucumber

300g (11oz) cherry tomatoes on the vine, quartered

1 bunch of coriander, chopped

Salt and freshly ground black pepper

1. Measure the sugar and vinegar into a small saucepan. Gently heat, stirring, until the sugar has dissolved. Pour into a bowl and set aside to cool.

2. Trim the fennel bulb and cut out the core, then slice the bulb into long, thin strips. Use a vegetable peeler to peel the cucumber lengthways in alternating strips, about 2cm (¾in) wide, to give a striped effect. Cut in half lengthways and use a teaspoon to remove the seeds, then cut into thick slices on the diagonal.

3. Tip the fennel strips and cucumber slices into the bowl with the dressing, toss together and marinate in the fridge for a minimum of an hour (see tip).

4. Add the tomato quarters, season with salt and pepper and add the chopped coriander. Toss everything together and tip on to a platter to serve.

PREPARE AHEAD

The fennel and cucumber can be left to marinate in the fridge up to 6 hours ahead, the tomatoes and coriander added to serve.

MARY'S EVERYDAY TIP

Pickling the fennel helps to tenderise it slightly and softens the aniseed flavour.

AVOCADO, ARTICHOKE AND FETA SALAD WITH ROASTED GRAPES

As delicious as it is impressive-looking, this salad is full of my favourite things – lovely as a light main meal. If you haven't roasted grapes before, they are a revelation! Some start to look like raisins and the flavour intensifies to give a sweetness that counteracts the saltiness of the feta perfectly.

SERVES 6 AS A SIDE AND 4 AS A MAIN DISH

COOK TIME: 15–20 MINUTES

200g (7oz) seedless black grapes

½ cucumber

200g (7oz) cherry tomatoes on the vine, halved

100g (4oz) lamb's lettuce

200g (7oz) chargrilled artichoke hearts in oil (drained weight), cut into eighths (see tip)

2 ripe avocados, peeled, diced and tossed in the juice of ½ lemon

200g (7oz) feta cheese, crumbled into large chunks (see tip)

6 spring onions, finely sliced

Salt and freshly ground black pepper

FOR THE DRESSING

1 tbsp Dijon mustard

90ml (3fl oz) good olive oil

1 tbsp white wine vinegar

Juice of ½ lemon

1 tbsp caster sugar

1. Preheat the oven to 200°C/180°C fan/Gas 6.

2. Arrange the grapes on a baking sheet and roast in the oven for about 15–20 minutes until soft.

3. Use a vegetable peeler to peel the cucumber lengthways in alternating strips, about 2cm (¾in) wide, to give a striped effect. Cut in half lengthways, then scoop out the seeds using a teaspoon and slice the flesh into horseshoe shapes.

4. To make the dressing, measure the ingredients into a bowl or small jug and whisk to combine (or place in a jar, screw on the lid and give a good shake).

5. When ready to serve, put the tomatoes and cucumber into a bowl and toss with half the dressing until coated. Scatter the lettuce over the base of a shallow, wide-based dish or platter, then scatter over the artichoke hearts, avocados and tomato cucumber mix, some salt and pepper to season, then the feta, spring onions and roasted grapes. Pour over the remaining dressing and serve.

PREPARE AHEAD

Assemble the salad up to 6 hours ahead, adding the avocado and dressing to serve.

The dressing can be made 2–3 days ahead.

MARY'S EVERYDAY TIPS

Chargrilled artichokes come in jars or chilled in tubs. Depending on the brand, they may already be cut into pieces.

Buy the best feta you can. It does vary in quality – the more delicate varieties tend to be less slimy and more crumbly, hence more delicious!

FENNEL AND WATERMELON SALAD WITH GOAT'S CHEESE BRUSCHETTA

A hearty mixed salad with tasty tomato and cheese-topped bruschetta, this is a complete meal in itself. Perfect for a summer lunch or picnic or as part of a spread for a party.

SERVES 6

COOK TIME:
18–20 MINUTES

FOR THE DRESSING

90ml (3fl oz) good olive oil

2 tbsp white wine vinegar

Juice and zest of ½ lemon

2 tsp runny honey

½ garlic clove, crushed

2 tsp chopped thyme leaves

1 fennel bulb, trimmed, cored and bulb finely chopped

FOR THE BRUSCHETTA

1 ciabatta loaf

3–4 tbsp olive oil

1 garlic clove, crushed

6 large ripe tomatoes, deseeded (see tip) and diced

1 heaped tbsp chopped thyme leaves

300g (11oz) soft goat's cheese, cut into thin slices

Salt and freshly ground black pepper

FOR THE SALAD

2 Little Gem lettuces, leaves sliced widthways into three

1 x 60g bag of lamb's lettuce

1 x 180g bag of lentil sprout mix (see tip on page 93)

1 cucumber, peeled, halved, deseeded and sliced on the diagonal

Flesh of ¼ watermelon, deseeded and sliced into small pieces

1 bunch of spring onions, sliced

1. Place all the dressing ingredients except the chopped fennel into a bowl and whisk to combine. Add the fennel, mixing it in well with the dressing to prevent it from discolouring, and leave to marinate for 30 minutes.

2. Preheat the oven to 220°C/200°C fan/Gas 7 or the grill to hot.

3. Next prepare the bruschetta. Cut the ciabatta into 12 slices on the diagonal. Mix the olive oil and garlic together in a small bowl. Brush both sides of the bread with the oil and garlic mixture and place on a baking sheet. Bake in the oven for 5 minutes, then turn the bread over and toast the other side for a further 4–5 minutes. Alternatively, toast under the grill.

4. Mix the diced tomatoes and thyme together in a bowl and season with salt and pepper (see tip). Spoon the mixture on top of the toasted pieces of bread. Arrange three slices of goat's cheese on top of each piece of bread and place on a baking sheet.

5. Bake the bruschetta for about 8 minutes in the hot oven, or brown under the grill, until crisp and lightly golden on top.

6. Meanwhile, mix the salad ingredients together in a large bowl or wide platter to show off the contrasting colours. Pour over the fennel and garlic dressing and toss together. Serve the salad with two bruschetta per person.

PREPARE AHEAD

Can be assembled up to 4 hours ahead and cooked in the oven or under the grill to serve. Or serve cold.

Assemble the salad up to 6 hours ahead; dress just before serving.

The dressing can be made up to 2 days ahead.

MARY'S EVERYDAY TIPS

Gone are the days when all watermelon were the size of your head. You can now buy mini watermelons perfect for this. Use half a small one for this recipe or a quarter of a large one.

If you have time, leave the tomatoes out at room temperature for 30 minutes once they are mixed with the thyme and seasoning – this will really enhance their flavour.

HERBED QUINOA AND BULGAR WHEAT SALAD WITH LEMON AND POMEGRANATE

I love the combination of bulgar wheat and quinoa – especially red quinoa with its russet colour – so it's great that you can now buy it in a mixed packet. Delicious with the fresh herbs and sun-blushed tomatoes stirred in. The pomegranate seeds aren't essential, but they add a lovely burst of freshness that complements the other ingredients. Serve as a side dish or as a salad for lunch.

SERVES 8 AS A SIDE AND 4–6 AS A MAIN DISH

COOK TIME: 20–25 MINUTES, PLUS STANDING

300g (11oz) bulgar wheat with mixed-colour quinoa (see tip)

1 tbsp olive oil

1 red onion, finely sliced

200g (7oz) sun-blushed tomatoes in oil (see tip on page 170), drained and cut in half

3 tbsp chopped mint

2 tbsp chopped flat-leaf parsley

3 tbsp finely snipped chives

2 tbsp torn basil leaves

100g (4oz) feta cheese, broken into pieces

50g (2oz) pomegranate seeds (optional)

Salt and freshly ground black pepper

FOR THE DRESSING

Juice and finely grated zest of 1 lemon

2 tbsp pomegranate syrup (see tip)

1 tsp sugar

2 tbsp good olive oil

1. Measure the mixed bulgar wheat and quinoa into a saucepan, pour in 500ml (18fl oz) of water and cover with a lid. Bring to the boil, then reduce the heat and simmer for 15–20 minutes – or according to the packet instructions. Remove from the heat and leave for about 10 minutes or until tender and all the liquid has been absorbed. Tip into a bowl and allow to cool.

2. To make the dressing, place the lemon juice and zest in a bowl or small jug, add the pomegranate syrup, sugar and olive oil and whisk together.

3. Place the 1 tablespoon of olive oil in a frying pan, add the onion and fry over a medium heat for 5–6 minutes. Tip into the bowl with the bulgar wheat and quinoa.

4. Add the sun-blushed tomatoes and herbs, season with salt and pepper and toss together. Pour on the dressing and mix well. Gently stir in the feta and the pomegranate seeds (if using), then check the seasoning, adding more salt and pepper to taste.

PREPARE AHEAD

Can be assembled up to 8 hours ahead – pour on the dressing up to 2 hours before serving.

MARY'S EVERYDAY TIPS

Replace with 150g (5oz) each of bulgar wheat and quinoa if buying in separate packets. See also tip on page 000.

A traditional ingredient in Middle Eastern cuisine, pomegranate syrup or molasses comes in a bottle and is available from most big supermarkets. It has a slightly sweet and sour taste that's perfect for dressings and sauces. If you are unable to find it, however, you could use pomegranate juice instead. The flavour is not as intense, but you could pop it in a saucepan and boil it until reduced to a thicker, syrupy consistency.

THREE BEETROOT SALAD WITH MOZZARELLA AND BASIL

A wonderfully fresh salad made using the finest ingredients, this looks stunning too with its amazing array of different colours. It would be great as a starter or to accompany a main dish. You can buy or grow many types of different beets, which give a lovely variety to any salad.

SERVES 6 AS A SIDE DISH OR STARTER

COOK TIME: 1 HOUR

550g (1lb 4oz) mixed small raw beetroot, such as red, yellow and candy-striped

250g (9oz) cherry tomatoes, halved

2 tbsp good olive oil

200g (7oz) mini mozzarella balls (drained weight), halved

Salt and freshly ground black pepper

TO SERVE

Sea salt flakes

1 handful of small basil leaves

1. Preheat the oven to 200°C/180°C fan/Gas 6.

2. Lay a sheet of foil in the base of a roasting tin – a sheet large enough to come up the sides of the tin – and sit the beetroot in the foil. Spoon over 4 tablespoons of water and season with salt and pepper, then wrap the foil over the top to make a parcel.

3. Bake in the oven for about 1 hour or until tender. Remove and set aside to cool.

4. Place the cherry tomatoes in a bowl, then pour over the olive oil and season with salt and pepper.

5. Once the beets are cool, peel with a small sharp knife (see tip) and cut into slices. Add to the bowl with the tomatoes and toss together.

6. To serve, tip the tomatoes and beetroot on to a serving platter, scatter over the mozzarella pieces (see tip) and sprinkle with sea salt and fresh basil leaves.

PREPARE AHEAD

Can be assembled up to 2 hours ahead.

The beetroot can be cooked up to 2 days ahead.

MARY'S EVERYDAY TIPS

Plastic gloves can be useful to stop the beetroot staining your hands when peeling them.

Scattering the mozzarella on top of the mixed tomatoes and beetroot helps to keep it looking white, providing a good colour contrast with the rest of the salad. Tossed with the other ingredients, the mozzarella soon turns pink otherwise.

WARM BULGAR WHEAT AND QUINOA BROCCOLI SALAD

Bulgar wheat and quinoa are often served cold, but they are equally lovely eaten warm, to go with roast chicken or fish. This salad is full of superfoods – not only delicious but super-healthy! It has a wonderful nutty flavour with a hint of chilli and added texture and colour from the vibrant green broccoli.

SERVES 6

COOK TIME:
25–30 MINUTES,
PLUS STANDING

175g (6oz) bulgar wheat

150g (5oz) mixed-colour quinoa (see tip)

2 fennel bulbs, trimmed, core removed and bulb thinly sliced

300g (11oz) tender-stem broccoli, stems chopped into 2cm (¾in) pieces

25g (1oz) butter

3 tbsp olive oil

2 large garlic cloves, crushed

Juice of 1 lemon and 1 lime

1–2 tsp harissa paste

1 large bunch of parsley, chopped

Salt and freshly ground black pepper

1. Measure the bulgar wheat and quinoa into a saucepan, add the 600ml (1 pint) of water and cover with a lid. Bring to the boil, then reduce the heat and simmer for 15–20 minutes – or according to the packet instructions. Remove from the heat and set aside for about 10 minutes or until tender and all the liquid has been absorbed.

2. Cook the fennel in boiling salted water for 3–4 minutes, then remove with a slotted spoon to a colander to drain and set aside. Add the broccoli to the pan and cook for 3 minutes. Drain and run for a second or two under cold water to stop it cooking further (see tip).

3. Heat the butter and oil in large frying pan over a high heat, and when the butter has melted, add the garlic and fennel and stir-fry for 3 minutes. Season with salt and pepper, then add the bulgar wheat and quinoa with the broccoli, citrus juices and harissa paste. Toss everything together until piping hot.

4. Stir in half the parsley, tip into a serving bowl and sprinkle with the rest.

PREPARE AHEAD

Can be cooked up to 4 hours ahead and pan-fried (with a little extra oil, if needed) to serve.

Leftovers can be kept overnight and served cold the next day.

MARY'S EVERYDAY TIPS

You can buy mixed packets of quinoa in different colours – red, black and white – from a supermarket or health-food shop. The individual types are otherwise available separately, white being the most common. You can also buy mixed packets of quinoa and bulgar wheat – perfect for the Herbed Quinoa and Bulgar Wheat Salad with Lemon and Pomegranate on page 217.

Running the broccoli under cold water sets the colour so it stays lovely and green.

CHICKEN SATAY SALAD

Light and fresh and a bit different, this is a great salad for a summer evening. The dressing has an Asian twist and is distinctly moreish. The chicken can be served warm, if you prefer.

**SERVES 6 AS
A MAIN DISH**

COOK TIME:
20–25 MINUTES

1 tbsp good olive oil

2 large skinless and boneless chicken breasts (about 200g/7oz each) (see tip)

4 Little Gem lettuces

3 spring onions, thinly sliced

100g (4oz) bean sprouts, rinsed

1 ripe avocado, peeled and sliced

1 tbsp chopped coriander

25g (1oz) salted peanuts, finely chopped

Salt and freshly ground black pepper

FOR THE DRESSING

1 garlic clove, crushed

½ fresh red chilli, deseeded and finely chopped

1 tbsp soy sauce

1 tbsp lime juice

3 tbsp peanut butter (smooth or crunchy – see tip)

3 tbsp good olive oil

1. Heat the oil in a griddle pan (see tip) and fry the chicken breasts for 10–12 minutes on each side until chargrilled and cooked through. Cook on a high heat initially, to brown the chicken, then lower the heat to ensure it cooks through. Test with a knife to check there are no pink juices. Remove from the pan and set aside to cool.

2. Meanwhile, remove any outer leaves from the Little Gem lettuces, trimming the root but keeping it intact, and cut lengthways into long thin strips through the root (effectively dividing each lettuce into eighths).

3. To make the dressing, measure all the ingredients into a bowl or small jug, add 4 tablespoons of water and whisk to combine (or place in a jar, screw on the lid and give a good shake).

4. To assemble the salad, arrange the strips of lettuce on a wide platter. Scatter with the spring onions, bean sprouts, avocado slices and coriander, then season with salt and pepper. Slice the chicken breasts into thick strips (ideally 12 in total, giving two per person) and scatter on top of the salad. Drizzle the dressing over the chicken and sprinkle with the peanuts.

5. Serve with any extra dressing on the side.

PREPARE AHEAD

Assemble up to 4 hours ahead, adding the avocado and dressing to serve.

The dressing can be made up to 3 days ahead.

MARY'S EVERYDAY TIPS

To help the chicken breasts cook quickly and evenly, place between sheets of greaseproof paper and bash with a rolling pin to make them an even thickness.

The dressing is fairly thick and the peanut butter helps to emulsify it. Smooth peanut butter will emulsify and thicken it more; crunchy will give more texture. It depends on preference and what you have to hand; either will work well. If you are using a sugar-free variety, add 1 tablespoon of honey to the dressing.

You can use a frying pan instead for this dish but a griddle pan gives lovely black chargrilled lines.

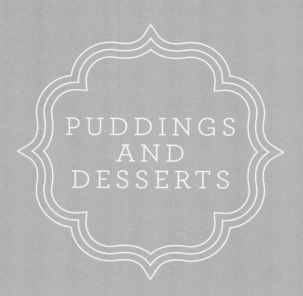

PUDDINGS
AND
DESSERTS

*There's always room
for something sweet at the end
of a meal, and whether it is a
comforting Classic Rice Pudding
(page 229) or a light and refreshing
bowl of Mango and Passion Fruit
Sorbet (page 252), a homemade
pudding is a treat for the
whole family.*

CLASSIC RICE PUDDING

Serve this with a bit of cream or a dollop of jam or syrup.
Or just enjoy on its own – it's delicious as it is!

SERVES 4–6

COOK TIME:
1¾–2 HOURS

Butter, for greasing

75g (3oz) pudding rice

900ml (1½ pints) full-fat
milk (see tip)

1 heaped tbsp caster sugar

1/2 tsp freshly grated
nutmeg (optional)

1. You will need a 1.6-litre (2¾-pint) wide-based ovenproof dish, well greased. Preheat the oven to 160°C/140°C fan/Gas 3.

2. Tip the rice into the dish. Heat the milk in a saucepan (see tip) and pour over the rice, then add the sugar and stir to combine.

3. Bake in the oven for about 30 minutes. Stir gently and sprinkle with a dusting of nutmeg, if you like. Continue cooking for a further 1¼–1½ hours until a golden skin has formed on top and the rice is soft and tender underneath. Serve hot.

MARY'S EVERYDAY TIPS

Full-fat milk gives the best rich flavour, though semi-skimmed would be fine too. If you only have semi-skimmed, add a little less and make up the full amount with cream.

Heating the milk gets the cooking going.

PEACH SPONGE PUDDING

An easy hot pudding – great for Sunday lunch. Just-ripe peaches are best for this dish – such as the firm 'home-ripening' kind sold in packs in the supermarket – as they will cook nicely and still keep their shape. Very juicy, ripe peaches would make the pudding batter wet and soggy. Nectarines or plums would also work well if fresh peaches are not available.

SERVES 6

COOK TIME:
50–60 MINUTES

175g (6oz) caster sugar

175g (6oz) butter, softened, plus extra for greasing

225g (8oz) self-raising flour

1 tsp baking powder

2 tsp vanilla extract (see tip)

3 eggs

3 just-ripe peaches (unpeeled), sliced

1 tbsp demerara sugar

1. You will need a 1.7-litre (3-pint) wide-based ovenproof dish. Preheat the oven to 180°C/160°C fan/Gas 4 and grease the dish with butter.

2. Measure the caster sugar, butter, flour, baking powder and vanilla extract into a large bowl, break in the eggs and beat well with an electric hand whisk until smooth and combined. Spoon into the prepared dish and level the top.

3. Arrange the peach slices in the dish and press slightly so they half sink into the mixture. Sprinkle with the demerara sugar.

4. Bake in the oven for 50–60 minutes until cooked through and golden brown on top. Slice into six squares and serve straight from the dish with custard or cream.

PREPARE AHEAD

Can be assembled up to 2 hours ahead, ready for the oven. Best eaten straight away as the peaches can turn a little grey otherwise.

MARY'S EVERYDAY TIPS

Use vanilla extract rather than essence, which is an artificial flavouring.

STEAMED GOLDEN APPLE PUDDING

This steamed pudding, with its delicious topping of apples and golden syrup, makes a lovely old-fashioned dessert – perfect for a chilly day. For a variation, try adding a teaspoon of ground ginger or cinnamon to the cake batter.

SERVES 6

COOK TIME:
2–2½ HOURS

1 large Bramley apple

150ml (5fl oz) golden syrup

175g (6oz) caster sugar

175g (6oz) butter, softened,
  plus extra for greasing

175g (6oz) self-raising flour

1 tsp baking powder

3 eggs

1. You will need a 1.1-litre (2-pint) pudding basin. Grease the basin with butter and place a square of foil in the base.

2. Peel and core the apple and cut into very small cubes. Place in a bowl, add 100ml (3½fl oz) of the golden syrup and mix well before tipping into the base of the pudding basin.

3. Measure the sugar, butter, flour and baking powder into a separate bowl and add the eggs, then use an electric hand whisk to beat until light and fluffy. Spoon the batter on top of the apple in the basin and level the top.

4. Cut out a piece of foil or baking paper a bit bigger than the top of the basin. Fold a pleat across the middle (see tip), butter the underside and sit on top of the basin. Crimp the foil or paper around the edge of the basin and seal with a large rubber band or tie with a piece of string.

5. Sit the basin in a deep saucepan (see tip), pour in enough boiling water to come halfway up and then bring to the boil on the hob. Lower the temperature and simmer for 2–2½ hours (topping up the water if needed) until the pudding is well risen and firm on top.

6. Take the basin out of the pan and remove the foil. Use a palette knife to loosen around the edges of the pudding, then invert on to a serving plate, carefully remove the basin and pour over the remaining golden syrup.

7. Serve hot with custard, cream or natural yoghurt.

PREPARE AHEAD

Can be made up to a day ahead and reheated to serve.

MARY'S EVERYDAY TIPS

The pleat in the foil is important, as this allows the foil/paper to stretch as the sponge rises.

For steaming the pudding, use a pan large enough that you can get your oven-gloved hands around the basin to lift it out. Check this before you fill it with boiling water!

PEAR AND APPLE CRUMBLE

Such a simple and delicious pud – maybe not for every day but definitely for a weekend treat! I have used eating apples for a change and because they hold their shape better when cooked. If you have a windfall of cooking apples, use them by all means, but you may need to add a little more sugar as they are sharper than dessert apples.

SERVES 4–6

COOK TIME:
45–50 MINUTES

FOR THE FILLING

25g (1oz) butter

1 tbsp muscovado sugar

6 eating apples, peeled,
  cored and cut into
  8 wedges lengthways

4 just-ripe pears, peeled,
  cored and cut into
  8 wedges lengthways

**FOR THE
CRUMBLE TOPPING**

150g (5oz) plain flour

50g (2oz) semolina (see tip)

25g (1oz) rolled oats

100g (4oz) cold butter, diced

60g (2½oz) caster sugar

1. You will need a 2-litre (3½-pint) wide-based ovenproof dish. Preheat the oven to 180°C/160°C fan/Gas 4.

2. To make the filling, melt the butter in a wide saucepan or a sauté pan, add the sugar and stir until dissolved. Add the apple wedges and toss over a high heat for about 2–3 minutes or until slightly golden. Use a slotted spoon to transfer the caramelised apples to the ovenproof dish. Cook the pears in the same way and add to the apples in the bowl. Mix together and then spread evenly over the base of the dish before leaving to cool (see tip).

3. Meanwhile, make the crumble topping, measure the flour, semolina and oats into a bowl. Rub in the butter until the mixture resembles breadcrumbs and then stir in the sugar.

4. Sprinkle the crumble in a thin layer over the top of the cooked apples and pears. Bake in the oven for about 45 minutes or until golden brown and bubbling. Serve with cream or custard.

PREPARE AHEAD

Can be made up to a day ahead, ready to cook.

Make the crumble mixture in advance and keep for 2–3 days in a sealed container in the fridge.

Make double quantities of the crumble and store what you don't use in the fridge so it can be used for a quick dessert.

FREEZE *Freezes well.*

MARY'S EVERYDAY TIPS

The semolina and oats give a lovely texture to the crumble. If semolina is not available, use ground rice instead.

The apples and pears need to cool down first or the raw crumble may start to melt and collapse into the hot fruit.

BLACKBERRY AND APPLE CRUMBLE PIE

This is a slightly different sort of pie as it has a pastry base and crumble topping; make in a traybake tin as it is then easy to cut into squares. Ideal for serving a crowd for Sunday lunch or for taking on a picnic and eating cold.

SERVES 8

COOK TIME:
40–45 MINUTES

**FOR THE
CRUMBLE TOPPING**

75g (3oz) butter, melted, plus extra for greasing

75g (3oz) self-raising flour

40g (1½oz) semolina (see tip)

40g (1½oz) caster sugar

**FOR THE
SHORTCRUST PASTRY**

175g (6oz) plain flour, plus extra for dusting

2 tbsp icing sugar

100g (4oz) cold butter, cubed

FOR THE FILLING

2 large Bramley apples, peeled, cored and coarsely grated

400g (14oz) blackberries

3 tbsp caster sugar

2 tbsp cornflour

1. You will need a 25 x 30cm (10 x 12in) traybake tin with 2cm (¾in) sides. Grease the tin with butter.

2. Measure all the ingredients for the crumble topping into a small bowl and mix with a table knife to combine. Use your hands to bring together into a ball. Wrap in cling film and place in the fridge to chill for a minimum of 30 minutes or until needed.

3. To make the pastry, measure the flour, icing sugar and butter into a food processor and whizz until the mixture resembles breadcrumbs. Alternatively, place the dry ingredients in a mixing bowl and rub in the butter with your fingertips. Add 1 tablespoon of cold water and pulse until smooth, adding another tablespoon of water if the dough seems too stiff. Roll into a ball, wrap in cling film and place in the fridge to chill for 30 minutes.

4. To make the filling, put the grated apple and the blackberries in a saucepan. Cover with a lid and simmer over a low heat for about 10 minutes. Tip the fruit into a sieve set over a bowl and use a wooden spoon to gently push all the liquid through the sieve, reserving the fruit (see tip).

5. Pour the liquid back into the pan, add the sugar and gently heat. Place the cornflour in a small bowl, add 1 tablespoon of water and mix until smooth. Add the cornflour mixture to the pan and quickly whisk until smooth and thickened. Remove from the heat, return the fruit to the pan and set aside to cool.

6. Preheat the oven to 200°C/180°C fan/Gas 6.

7. Roll out the chilled pastry on a floured worktop into a rectangle slightly bigger all round than the tin – with enough to come up the sides and overlap it slightly – and the thickness of a £1 coin. Line the tin with the pastry, crimping around the top edge and pricking the base with a fork.

8. Line with baking paper and add some baking beans, then bake blind in the oven for about 10–15 minutes (see tip on page 240). Remove the beans and paper and return to the oven for a further 5 minutes. Add the cold filling and spread out over the base of the pastry in the tin.

Recipe continues overleaf

9. Coarsely grate the chilled crumble topping all over the top, covering the fruit filling well (see tip). Bake for a further 15 minutes until golden.

10. Set aside to cool a little, then cut into 8 portions (by making one cut lengthways across the mixture and four widthways) and serve hot with custard or ice cream.

PREPARE AHEAD

Can be made up to a day ahead and reheated.

FREEZE *The cooked dish freezes well.*

MARY'S EVERYDAY TIPS

If you can't get semolina, use ground rice instead.

It is important to drain the cooked fruit and thicken the liquid with cornflour; this prevents the pastry from having a soggy bottom!

Cover the fruit filling well with the crumble mix, right to the edges of the pastry case, so that the filling doesn't scorch while baking.

PROFITEROLES WITH WARM CHOCOLATE FUDGE SAUCE

Such a favourite with everyone and even more irresistible with this warm chocolate sauce. It's not as smooth as the classic sauce, but has a wonderful caramel and chocolate flavour and a divine fudgy texture.

MAKES 30 PROFITEROLES

COOK TIME:
30–35 MINUTES, PLUS COOLING

FOR THE CHOUX PASTRY

75g (3oz) butter, cubed

100g (4oz) strong white flour, sifted

3 eggs, beaten

FOR THE CREAM FILING

500ml (18fl oz) pouring double cream

1 tsp vanilla extract

FOR THE SAUCE

100g (4oz) butter

200g (7oz) light muscovado sugar

125ml (4fl oz) pouring double cream

100g (4oz) dark chocolate, broken into rough chunks

1. You will need a piping bag fitted with a plain nozzle. Preheat the oven to 220°C/200°C fan/Gas 7 and line two baking sheets with baking paper.

2. First make the choux pastry. Place the butter in a saucepan and pour in 200ml (7fl oz) of water. Slowly bring to the boil. Tip the flour on to a sheet of paper. Remove the pan from the heat and immediately pour the flour in, then beat with a wooden spoon until the mixture comes together in a ball. Return to the heat and continue to beat for 1 minute. Set aside to cool for 2–3 minutes. Gradually add the beaten eggs, beating as you add them until the mixture is glossy, smooth and stiff.

3. Spoon into a piping bag and pipe 30 walnut-sized balls on to the lined baking sheets, spacing them evenly apart.

4. Bake in the oven for 10 minutes, then lower the temperature to 180°C/160°C fan/Gas 4 and cook for a further 10 minutes. Remove from the oven, use a sharp knife to make a hole in the base, or side, of each profiterole (large enough to insert the piping nozzle) and return to the oven, hole side up, for a further 10 minutes to dry them out. Remove from the oven and transfer to a wire rack to cool.

5. Pour the cream into a bowl, add the vanilla extract and whisk into soft peaks. Fill a piping bag with the whipped cream and pipe a little into each cooled profiterole. Chill in the fridge until needed.

6. To make the sauce, heat the butter, sugar and cream in a saucepan over a gentle heat. Stir until smooth then increase the heat and boil for 1–2 minutes. Add the chocolate and stir until melted and the mixture is smooth and shiny.

7. Arrange the profiteroles in a bowl and pour over the warm sauce to serve.

PREPARE AHEAD

The profiteroles can be filled up to 4 hours ahead and served with the hot sauce. If serving cold, they can be dipped in the hot sauce and set aside for up to 4 hours ahead.

MARY'S EVERYDAY TIP

Have the flour weighed out and ready to hand by the hob, as it needs to be tipped in very quickly. And beat hard once it's been added. This ensures that the profiteroles will rise well.

APPLE AND LEMON GALETTE

Think of a cross between tarte au citron and a delicate French apple pastry, and you have this! The crisp pastry, fresh lemon cream and thin apple slices are such a delicious combination. The long shape of the tin – known as a tranche tin – makes it a bit special too. I have used the same type of tin for my Plum Tomato, Olive and Marjoram Tart on page 175. If you don't have a tranche tin, a 20cm (8in) deep, round flan tin would make a good alternative otherwise.

SERVES 6

COOK TIME:
40–45 MINUTES

FOR THE PASTRY

150g (5oz) plain flour, plus extra for dusting

75g (3oz) cold butter, cubed

25g (1oz) icing sugar

1 egg, beaten

FOR THE FILLING

150ml (5fl oz) double cream

100g (4oz) caster sugar

2 eggs, lightly beaten

Juice and finely grated zest of 1 lemon

2 red eating apples

2 tbsp apricot jam, to glaze

1. You will need a 12 x 36cm (5 x 14in) loose-bottomed, fluted tranche tin with 2.5–3cm (1–1¼in) sides.

2. To make the pastry, measure the flour, butter and sugar into a food processor and whizz until the mixture is like breadcrumbs. Alternatively, place the dry ingredients in a mixing bowl and rub in the butter with your fingertips. Add the egg and whizz again until a ball of dough is formed.

3. Roll out on a floured work surface to the thickness of a £1 coin and large enough to fit the tin (see tips on page 176). Line the base and sides of the tin, leaving a generous edge to allow for shrinkage in the oven. Prick the pastry all over with a fork and chill in the fridge for 30 minutes.

4. Meanwhile, preheat the oven to 200°C/180°C fan/Gas 6 and place a large baking sheet inside to get very hot.

5. To make the filling, measure the cream and sugar into a jug, add the eggs and the lemon juice and zest and whisk well together.

6. Line the pastry case with baking paper and baking beans, place on the hot baking sheet and bake blind for 15 minutes (see tip). Remove the paper and beans and return to the oven for a further 5 minutes to dry out.

7. While the pastry is baking, core the apples (keeping them unpeeled) and slice very thinly.

8. Remove the pastry case from the oven and lower the oven temperature to 180°C/160°C fan/Gas 4.

9. Pour the lemon cream into the pastry case. Arrange the thin slices of apple in six neat rows across the width of the tart, so that, when cut, each slice of the galette has its own fan of apple on top. Bake in the oven for 20–25 minutes or until golden. The apples should be just softened and the filling just set (see tip).

Recipe continues overleaf

10. Set aside to cool for 5 minutes, then trim the edges to remove any overhanging pastry. Heat the apricot jam with 1 tablespoon of water and pour through a sieve to remove any lumps. Carefully brush over the apple slices to give an even glaze.

11. Carefully remove from the tin and serve warm, sliced between the apple fans, with cream poured over.

PREPARE AHEAD

Can be made up to 6 hours ahead and gently reheated to serve.

MARY'S EVERYDAY TIPS

Baking blind is important to ensure that the pastry is completely cooked and crisp and does not become soggy when the filling is added. If you don't have ceramic baking beans, use dried beans or lentils or uncooked rice.

Don't overbake the galette or the filling may curdle.

STICKY TOFFEE PUDDING

An everyday classic that always goes down well. I like to serve a large, family-sized version of the pudding and spoon or cut it into squares to serve. For true addicts, see also page 280 for sticky toffee pudding transformed into cupcakes!

SERVES 6–8

COOK TIME:
35–40 MINUTES

FOR THE PUDDING

100g (4oz) butter, softened, plus extra for greasing

175g (6oz) light muscovado sugar (see tip)

225g (8oz) self-raising flour

1 tsp baking powder

1 tsp bicarbonate of soda

3 tbsp black treacle (see tip on page 000)

2 eggs

275ml (9½fl oz) milk

FOR THE TOFFEE SAUCE

100g (4oz) butter

125g (4oz) light muscovado sugar

1 tbsp black treacle

300ml (10fl oz) pouring double cream

1 tsp vanilla extract

1. You will need a 1.75-litre (3-pint) wide-based, shallow ovenproof dish. Preheat the oven to 180°C/160°C fan/Gas 4 and grease the dish with butter.

2. Measure the butter and sugar into a large bowl with the flour, baking powder, bicarbonate of soda and treacle (see tip), and add the eggs. Whisk using an electric hand whisk for about 30 seconds or until combined. Gradually pour in the milk and whisk until smooth. Expect it to have a slightly curdled look.

3. Pour the batter into the prepared dish and bake in the oven for 35–40 minutes or until well risen and springing up in the centre.

4. Meanwhile make the sauce. Measure all the ingredients into a saucepan and stir over a low heat until the butter has melted and the sugar is dissolved. Bring to the boil and cook, stirring, for a few minutes until thickened.

5. To serve, pour half the sauce over the pudding when it comes out of the oven and serve the rest in a jug on the side. Serve with cream or ice cream.

PREPARE AHEAD

Can be cooked up to a day ahead and reheated.

The sauce can be made up to 3 days ahead.

MARY'S EVERYDAY TIP

Muscovado sugar is unrefined sugar made from sugar cane and, with its fudgy, lightly caramel flavour, it is perfect for this recipe. For a stronger toffee taste, closer to the liquorice flavour of black treacle, you could use dark muscovado sugar instead.

WHITE CHOCOLATE
AND RASPBERRY CHEESECAKE

This smooth and creamy cheesecake is delicious: the digestive biscuits and white chocolate give sweetness, while the raspberry coulis provides a lovely sharp contrast, in colour as well as taste. Filling the holes in the middle of the topping with the coulis means there is a lovely surprise when you cut into it – creating a two-tone effect but a bit different from a rippled cheesecake.

SERVES 6–8

PREP TIME: 30 MINUTES, PLUS CHILLING

FOR THE BASE

150g (5oz) digestive biscuits

60g (2 1/2oz) butter, plus extra for greasing

1 tbsp demerara sugar

FOR THE TOPPING

200g (7oz) white chocolate

1 x 250g tub of full-fat mascarpone cheese

300ml (10fl oz) pouring double cream

1 tsp vanilla extract

500g (15oz) fresh raspberries

1 tbsp icing sugar

1. You will need a 20cm (8in) round spring-form tin with deep sides, and a piping bag fitted with a plain nozzle (optional). Butter the base of the tin and line with a disc of baking paper.

2. To make the base, measure the biscuits into a resealable freezer bag and use a rolling pin, or the base of a saucepan, to crush into fine crumbs, but still with a bit of texture.

3. Heat the butter in a small saucepan over a low heat until just melted. Add the crushed biscuits and sugar and stir until combined. Spoon into the base of the prepared tin and press with the back of a spoon until level. Chill in the fridge while you make the topping.

4. Break the chocolate into a separate bowl (see tip), and sit it on top of a pan of simmering water. Stir until melted but not hot, then leave to cool down for 5–10 minutes until cool but still liquid.

5. Meanwhile, tip the mascarpone into a bowl, and mix with a spatula to loosen so it is soft. Stir in the cream and vanilla extract, stirring with the spatula until smooth.

6. To make a coulis for the top of the cheesecake, place half the raspberries into a small blender or food processor. Add the icing sugar and whizz until runny, then pour through a sieve to remove the seeds.

7. Pour the melted chocolate into the bowl with the mascarpone mixture and stir to combine, taking care not to over-mix.

8. Spoon half the white chocolate mixture on to the biscuit base in the tin. Use the handle of a teaspoon to make a few small holes in the white chocolate mixture, pushing right down to the top of the biscuit base.

Recipe continues overleaf

9. Pour or pipe enough of the coulis into the holes to fill them, setting aside the remaining coulis for decorating the top of the cheesecake. Spoon the remaining white chocolate mixture on top and smooth and level the top. Cover with cling film and chill in the fridge for a minimum of 6 hours or ideally overnight.

10. To serve, arrange the rest of the raspberries on top of the cheesecake and drizzle over the remaining coulis. Run a palette knife around the edges of the tin before removing the sides and base (see tip), and sit it on a serving plate.

PREPARE AHEAD

Can be made up to 2 days ahead and kept in the fridge. Decorate just before serving for the best results.

FREEZE *Freezes well without the raspberries and coulis on top.*

MARY'S EVERYDAY TIPS

To break the chocolate easily, leave it in the wrapper and give a sharp tap on the work surface before unwrapping the broken pieces.

Carefully run the palette knife under the biscuit base to release, or keep the cheesecake on the base of the tin if you prefer.

RHUBARB AND GINGER ICE CREAM

Rhubarb and ginger are a winning combination in this delicious homemade ice cream. If you can't get pink rhubarb, the more mature green stalks are fine, though the tender pink stems do make a lovely-coloured purée to swirl through the ice cream. Crystallised ginger could be used instead of the stem ginger, if not available.

MAKES ABOUT 2 LITRES (3½ PINTS)

COOK TIME: 10 MINUTES, PLUS FREEZING

225g (8oz) caster sugar

800g (1¾lb) pink rhubarb stalks, sliced into 2cm (¾in) pieces

4 eggs, separated

300ml (10fl oz) double cream

8 stem ginger bulbs, chopped

1. You will need a 2-litre (3½-pint) freezer-proof container with a lid.

2. Measure 125g (4½oz) of the sugar into a shallow saucepan and add 3–4 tablespoons of water. Stir slowly over a low heat until the sugar has dissolved and the liquid is clear.

3. Add the rhubarb and stir over a medium heat until simmering. Cover the pan with a lid, reduce the heat to low and gently simmer for 4–5 minutes or until tender. Using a slotted spoon, scoop out the rhubarb into a sieve set over a bowl to drain the syrup. Purée half the rhubarb chunks in a blender until smooth, then set aside to cool (see tips). Reserve the syrup and the remaining chunky rhubarb to serve as a compote alongside the ice cream.

4. Place the egg whites in a large, spotlessly clean bowl and use an electric hand whisk to whisk into stiff peaks. Gradually add the remaining sugar, still whisking on maximum speed, until fully incorporated and the mixture is glossy.

5. In a separate bowl, whip the cream to soft peaks, then stir in the egg yolks. Carefully fold in the egg whites until smooth and combined. Stir in the puréed rhubarb and chopped ginger to give a ripple effect. Spoon into the freezer-proof container, cover with the lid and freeze for a minimum of 8 hours or overnight.

6. Remove from the freezer 15 minutes before serving. Scoop out the ice cream and serve with the compote.

PREPARE AHEAD

Can be made up to a month ahead (both the ice cream and the compote) and kept in the freezer.

MARY'S EVERYDAY TIPS

It is important to purée the rhubarb before adding it to the ice cream as chunks of rhubarb would crystallise if frozen within the ice cream.

Make sure the rhubarb purée has cooled down fully before adding it to the whipped cream and egg mixture. If it is still warm, the heat will cause all the air to be lost from the mixture.

MELON AND PINEAPPLE SALAD WITH LIME SYRUP

A very simple fruit salad, and so quick to make – this would be just the thing to serve a crowd alongside a naughty dessert! The addition of the passion fruit really lifts the flavours and the lime in the syrup adds an extra zing. This recipe works best with lovely ripe, juicy fruit. If buying from a supermarket, where it is often chilled and under-ripe, buy a day or two in advance before making the recipe, and let it ripen and gain flavour at home.

SERVES 6

COOK TIME: 5 MINUTES

1 pineapple, peeled, cored and cut into large chunks

1 ripe cantaloupe melon, peeled, deseeded and cut into large chunks (see tip)

2 ripe passion fruit (see tip)

FOR THE SYRUP

100g (4oz) caster sugar

Juice and finely grated zest of 1 lime

1. To make the syrup, measure the sugar and 150ml (5fl oz) of water into a saucepan. Stir over a low heat until the sugar has dissolved and the liquid is clear. Remove the spoon from the pan, then turn up the heat and boil until slightly reduced and syrupy but still clear. Set aside to cool down a little, then stir in the lime juice and zest.

2. Arrange the pineapple and melon pieces in a bowl. Cut the passion fruit in half, scoop out the pulp and add to the bowl. Pour over the lime syrup and stir to mix.

PREPARE AHEAD

Can be made up to 12 hours ahead.

MARY'S EVERYDAY TIPS

Use a different type of melon, if you like, though the orange-fleshed ones look the most attractive with the paler pineapple.

Passion fruit are often sold under-ripe (with smooth skins). They are at their sweetest once the skin has become wrinkled and gnarled, so pick out ones like this if you can.

MANGO AND PASSION FRUIT SORBET WITH MINT SALSA

Sorbet is so refreshing and makes a change from ice cream. No special ice-cream machine is needed – just a food processor and a freezer! For the best flavour, the mangos should be ripe, however. When buying, check that they're wrinkled, sweet-smelling and soft to the touch.

MAKES ABOUT 1.1 LITRES (2 PINTS)

COOK TIME: 15 MINUTES, PLUS FREEZING

225g (8oz) caster sugar

6 ripe passion fruit

Juice of 3 limes

350g (12oz) ripe mango flesh (from about 2 large mangos)

FOR THE MINT SALSA

120g (4oz) caster sugar

2 ripe passion fruit

Juice of 2 limes

1 tbsp chopped mint, plus extra sprigs to decorate

1. You will need a 1.1-litre (2-pint) freezer-proof container with a lid.

2. First make a syrup. Measure the caster sugar and 150ml (5fl oz) of cold water into a saucepan. Stir over a low heat until the sugar has dissolved and the liquid is clear. Remove the spoon from the pan, then raise the heat and boil until the liquid has reduced by half. The syrup will be thickened and slightly sticky. Remove from the heat and add a further 450ml (15fl oz) of cold water. Set aside.

3. Cut the passion fruit in half and scoop out the pulp. Place the pulp in a sieve set over a jug and use a spoon to push through as much juice as possible. Pour in the lime juice. It should measure about 150ml (5fl oz) in total. If there isn't quite enough liquid, try pushing out more of the juice from the pulp in the sieve (see tip).

4. Purée the mango flesh until smooth in a food processor or using a hand blender. Add the syrup to the mango purée and whizz again, then stir in the mixed passion fruit and lime juice. Pour into the freezer-proof container, cover with the lid and freeze for minimum of 8 hours or ideally overnight.

5. When the sorbet is frozen, remove from the freezer and leave to stand for 10–15 minutes to soften slightly. Spoon chunks of frozen sorbet into a food processor and whizz to break up the sugar crystals, so the sorbet is smooth with a creamy texture (see tip). Spoon back into the container and freeze until needed.

6. To make the salsa, measure the sugar and 150ml (5fl oz) of water into a saucepan. Stir over a low heat until the sugar has dissolved, then raise the heat and boil for 3 minutes, to make a syrup. Cut the passion fruit in half, scoop out the pulp (see tip) and add to a bowl with the lime juice. Leave to cool, then add the chopped mint (see tip).

Recipe continues overleaf

7. Take the sorbet out of the freezer 15 minutes before serving to make it easier to remove from the container. Scoop into balls and spoon over a little mint salsa. For extra-special presentation, make a pyramid shape from the balls and pour the salsa over the top. Decorate with sprigs of mint.

PREPARE AHEAD

The sorbet can be made up to a month ahead and kept frozen. You could also ball up the sorbet and freeze the balls solid to save time on the day you intend to serve it.

Make the salsa up to a week ahead and add the mint on the day of serving.

MARY'S EVERYDAY TIPS

For an impressive crowd, double the mixture for an extra-large pyramid!

Whizzing the frozen sorbet to break up the crystals is a key step. It really alters the texture and colour of the sorbet, making it much smoother as well as pale and creamy. If your food processor is too full, it won't blend the sorbet thoroughly, so do it in batches if needed, and re-blitz any larger frozen lumps that may remain after the first whizz.

You can whizz the pulp in a mini food processor first, if you like, as this helps to extract more juice.

Do not add the fresh mint to the warm liquid or it will discolour.

PARIS-BREST WITH DOUBLE CHOCOLATE

Created in the early twentieth century to commemorate the Paris-Brest cycle race, this classic French dessert is one of my favourites. Made in a ring (to represent a bicycle wheel!), it's quicker to fill than lots of individual éclairs or profiteroles (see page 239) if you are entertaining. The cooking time is longer, but the choux ring can be made well in advance and, filled with whipped cream and topped with the chocolate ganache, it looks most impressive!

SERVES 10–12

COOK TIME:
11/4–11/2 HOURS,
PLUS COOLING

150g (5oz) dark chocolate, broken into chunks

600ml (1 pint) double cream

50g (2oz) white chocolate, broken into chunks

Icing sugar, for dusting

FOR THE CHOUX PASTRY

100g (4oz) butter, cubed

1 tsp caster sugar

150g (5oz) strong white flour

4 eggs, beaten

1. You will need a piping bag fitted with a plain nozzle (or snip off the end of the bag). Preheat the oven to 220°C/200°C fan/Gas 7 and line a baking sheet with baking paper.

2. First make the choux pastry. Measure the butter and sugar into a saucepan, pour in 250ml (9fl oz) of water and slowly bring to the boil. Tip the flour on to a sheet of baking paper. As soon as the mixture starts to boil, remove from the heat and shoot the flour into the pan, then beat with a wooden spoon until the mixture comes together in a ball (see tip on page 239). Return to the heat and continue to beat for 1 minute. Set aside to cool for 2–3 minutes.

3. Gradually add the beaten eggs, little by little, beating as you add them until the mixture is glossy, smooth and stiff. Place in the piping bag.

4. Draw a 20cm (8in) circle on the baking paper lining the baking sheet – a cake tin makes a good template. Pipe a ring of choux dough on top, about 4cm (1½in) thick, building up the layers until the batter is used up. Alternatively, make a ring by adding spoonfuls of the mixture to the lined baking sheet and using the back of your spoon to smooth the mixture together.

5. Bake in the oven for 20 minutes, then turn down the heat to 180°C/160°C fan/Gas 4 and bake for another 40–50 minutes until crisp, dry and lightly golden (see tip). Remove from the oven and use a sharp knife to pierce the sides of the choux ring before returning to the oven, with the heat turned off and the door left slightly ajar, to dry out for 10–20 minutes as the oven cools (see tip). Remove from the oven and leave to cool on a wire rack.

Recipe continues overleaf

6. Meanwhile, make the ganache. Place the dark chocolate and 150ml (5fl oz) of the cream in a bowl set over a pan of simmering water. When the chocolate has melted, set aside to cool and thicken to the consistency of thin mayonnaise. Place the white chocolate in a separate bowl set over a pan of simmering water and allow to melt just enough to be lukewarm. If too hot it will not set.

7. Pour the remaining 450ml (15fl oz) of cream into a bowl and whip into soft peaks. When the choux ring is completely cold, slice in half horizontally and transfer the bottom half to a large serving plate. Spoon the whipped cream into this half.

8. Drizzle about a quarter of the cooled dark chocolate ganache on top of the cream-filled base. Carefully sit the top section of the choux ring on top and spoon over the remaining ganache in a zigzag pattern (see tip). Drizzle over the white chocolate to decorate, and dust with icing sugar. Chill in the fridge before serving.

PREPARE AHEAD

Can be assembled up to 2 hours ahead.

The choux ring can be made up to 8 hours ahead.

MARY'S EVERYDAY TIPS

Don't be tempted to open the oven door too soon or the choux pastry will deflate.

It's important to dry out the choux ring so that it's not doughy inside.

When covering the Paris–Brest with the ganache, place over a tray lined with baking paper to catch any excess and leave to firm up or it will be tricky to move. If any ganache is left over after icing the choux ring, simply pour into a jug to serve separately.

MOJITO CHEESECAKES

This elegant-looking, light cheesecake served in cocktail glasses has a lovely almond-flavoured crunch from the amaretti biscuits and a nice boozy kick! Quick and easy to prepare, it is ideal for rounding off a meal.

SERVES 6

PREP TIME:
20 MINUTES,
PLUS CHILLING

25g (1oz) butter

60g (2½oz) amaretti biscuits

100g (4oz) full-fat
  cream cheese

150ml (5fl oz) double cream

Scant 2 tbsp white rum

25g (1oz) icing sugar, sifted

Juice and finely grated zest
  of 1 large lime

Mint, lemon verbena or
  lemon balm leaves,
  to decorate

1. You will need six glasses or ramekins, each around 100ml (3fl oz) in capacity. I like to use Martini-style glasses as they give a nice shape.

2. Melt the butter in a saucepan and remove from the heat. Place the amaretti in a resealable freezer bag and bash with a rolling pin, or with the base of another saucepan, to finely crush. Reserve 2 tablespoons to decorate, then tip the rest into the pan with the melted butter and stir to combine. Divide the coated biscuit crumbs between the glasses or ramekins (about 1 tablespoon per glass) and press down slightly.

3. To make the filling, soften the cream cheese in a bowl and mix in the cream until smooth and well combined. Add the rum and icing sugar and most of the lime zest, reserving some for decoration, and mix well. Add the lime juice and mix again. The mixture will thicken instantly. Spoon this on top of the biscuit bases in the glasses.

4. Sprinkle the remaining biscuit crumbs and lime zest over each and garnish with a sprig of mint, lemon verbena or lemon balm. Chill in the fridge until ready to serve.

PREPARE AHEAD

The cheesecake can be made up to 2 days ahead and kept in the fridge, but serve at room temperature or it will be too firm. Decorate with the crushed biscuits and herb sprigs just before serving.

MARY'S EVERYDAY TIP

'Scant' means just under 2 tablespoons here, but add a little more rum (just enough to avoid making the mixture sloppy) if you like it fiery!

CHOCOLATE AND HAZELNUT TORTE

Layers of chocolate sponge sandwiched together with whipped cream and chocolate ganache, this impressive dessert would be perfect for a special supper. It can be prepared well in advance, kept hidden in the fridge and brought out to general applause!

SERVES 6–8

COOK TIME:
15–20 MINUTES,
PLUS COOLING

**FOR THE
CHOCOLATE SPONGE**

Butter, for greasing

175g (6oz) dark chocolate, broken into pieces

6 eggs, separated

175g (6oz) caster sugar

2 tbsp cocoa powder

4 tbsp brandy, for brushing

FOR THE GANACHE

150g (5oz) dark chocolate, broken into pieces

150ml (5fl oz) double cream

50g (2oz) toasted chopped hazelnuts (see tip on page 296)

FOR THE FILLING

200ml (7fl oz) double cream

1 tsp vanilla extract

1. You will need a 23 x 30cm (9 x 12in) Swiss roll tin. Preheat the oven to 180°C/160°C fan/Gas 4, then grease the tin with butter and line with baking paper.

2. First make the sponge. Place the chocolate in a bowl set over a pan of simmering water and stir until just melted. Set aside for a few minutes to cool (see tip).

3. Place the egg yolks and caster sugar in a large bowl. Using an electric hand whisk, beat at a high speed until fluffy and pale cream in colour and the 'ribbon' stage has been reached (see tip). Stir the cooled chocolate into the whisked mixture.

4. In a separate, spotlessly clean bowl, whisk the egg whites into soft peaks, like a cloud. Stir one large tablespoon of the whisked egg whites into the creamy chocolate mixture and mix to loosen. Carefully cut and fold in the remaining egg whites until evenly mixed. Sift in the cocoa powder and carefully stir in until the mixture is evenly coloured throughout.

5. Spoon into the prepared tin and level the top. Bake in the oven for 15–20 minutes or until well risen, springy to the touch and with a slight crust on top. Leave to cool for 10 minutes in the tin. Lay a sheet of baking paper on a work surface, invert the sponge on to the paper and then carefully remove the lining paper from the bottom of the cake. Brush the sponge with the brandy and leave until stone cold.

6. To make the ganache, put the chocolate into a bowl set over a pan of simmering water. Add the cream and stir until the mixture is runny, smooth and combined. Set aside to cool for 20–30 minutes.

7. Cut the cold sponge into three strips lengthways. Whip the cream for the filling into soft peaks and stir in the vanilla extract. Use a palette knife to transfer one strip of sponge on to a long plate (see tip).

Recipe continues overleaf

8. Spread half the whipped cream on top, drizzle with a little ganache and sit another piece of sponge on top. Add the rest of the cream, drizzle with more of the ganache and top with the third strip of sponge. Spread the remaining ganache on top and sprinkle with the toasted chopped hazelnuts. Cut widthways into slices and serve.

PREPARE AHEAD

Can be assembled up to 6 hours ahead and kept chilled until ready to serve.

MARY'S EVERYDAY TIPS

The chocolate must be cooled before being added to the whisked mixture; if it is too hot, it will cause all the air that has just been incorporated to escape.

The whisked sponge mixture must reach the 'ribbon' stage before the cooled chocolate is added. This is when the trail can be seen on the surface when the whisk beaters are lifted. Another tip is to make a figure of eight with the trail of batter from the beaters. If it stays on the surface long enough to see the '8', then the batter is thick enough.

When assembling the torte layers, it's best to do this on the serving plate or board, as once the torte has been assembled, it is harder to lift neatly.

PASSION FRUIT AND BANANA ETON MESS

Such a quick pudding and sure to please. The sharpness of the passion fruit counteracts the sweetness of the meringue and richness of the cream, while the banana adds bulk. If you are not keen on banana, however, you can replace it with 100g (4oz) seedless white grapes, cut in half, or a similar quantity of chopped mango. Either of these would work really well too.

SERVES 6

PREP TIME:
20 MINUTES

300ml (10fl oz) pouring double cream

200g (7oz) natural Greek-style yoghurt

3 ripe passion fruit (see tip on page 250)

4 tbsp passion fruit purée (see tip)

1 large just-ripe banana, peeled and sliced

10 ready-made meringue nests, broken into large pieces

TO DECORATE

2 ready-made meringue nests

1 ripe passion fruit, sliced into thin wedges

2 tbsp passion fruit purée

6 mint sprigs

1. You will need six glasses or similar receptacles, each 150–200ml (5–7fl oz) in capacity. I like to use small tumblers or saucer champagne glasses.

2. Measure the double cream into a large bowl and whisk into soft peaks, then stir in the yoghurt. Halve the passion fruit, scoop out the pulp and add to the cream with the passion fruit purée. Add the banana slices and broken meringues and gently fold together.

3. Divide the mixture between the glasses, shaping the top of the mixture into a peak with your spoon. Chill in the fridge until ready to serve.

4. Shortly before serving, slice the meringues into shards and insert into the top of each glass. Garnish with a couple of passion fruit wedges, a drizzle of passion fruit purée and a sprig of mint.

PREPARE AHEAD

Best made up to 4 hours ahead (the meringue dissolves if left much longer). Make sure the banana is not in contact with the air or it may discolour.

MARY'S EVERYDAY TIPS

Passion fruit purée is now easy to buy and is so useful! If you are unable to find it, however, look for passion fruit syrup or coulis instead. Alternatively, use the fresh fruit: scoop out the pulp, purée in a food processor and push through a sieve to remove the seeds. (One passion fruit yields about 20ml/¾fl oz of juice/purée, so you would need four to five fresh fruit for this recipe.)

RAINBOW MERINGUES

Crisp on the outside and with lovely distinctive flavours, these coloured small meringues are as delicious as they are decorative. Served in a bowl with whipped cream and fruit on the side, they would be great for a party.

MAKES 50–60 MERINGUES DEPENDING ON VOLUME (ABOUT 12–15 OF EACH COLOUR)

COOK TIME: 45–50 MINUTES

4 egg whites (see tip)

225g (8oz) white caster sugar (see tip)

1 tbsp freeze-dried raspberries

¼ tsp instant coffee granules

Finely grated zest of ½ lemon

5g (¼oz) pistachio nuts, finely chopped

Yellow, pink and green food gels

1. You will need a piping bag fitted with a plain nozzle. Preheat the oven to 140°C/120°C fan/Gas 1 and line two large baking sheets with baking paper (a blob of meringue underneath will help to hold it down before piping).

2. Place the egg whites in a bowl and whisk on full speed until stiff like a fluffy cloud. Still whisking on full speed, add the sugar, little at a time, until the mixture is thick and glossy. Divide the meringue equally between four small bowls. Set aside and cover while mixing the four different flavours.

3. To make raspberry meringues, add six drops of pink gel and 1 tablespoon of freeze-dried raspberries to one of the four bowls. Stir gently to colour and give a light ripple effect, and spoon into a piping bag.

4. To make coffee meringues, mix the coffee granules with ½ teaspoon of hot water to dissolve. Allow to cool slightly before adding to a second bowl of meringue. Mix together and spoon into another piping bag.

5. To make lemon meringues, add the lemon zest and six drops of yellow gel to another bowl. Stir through lightly to colour and to give a ripple effect, and spoon into another piping bag.

6. To make pistachio meringues, add the nuts and ripple six drops of green gel through the meringue in the fourth bowl, then spoon into a fourth piping bag.

7. Pipe 15 tiny blobs, about 4cm (1.5in) in diameter, of each type of meringue on to the baking sheets. Bake in the oven for 45–50 minutes until they are just firm and easy to remove from the baking sheets. Cool on a wire rack.

PREPARE AHEAD

Can be made up to a month ahead and stored in an airtight container.

MARY'S EVERYDAY TIPS

Keep leftover egg yolks in the fridge for up to 2 days. To stop them drying out, cover with a little water and drain it off before using. Two can be saved to use for the Griddled Chicken Carbonara recipe on page 000, for example.

Don't use golden caster sugar; this gives a lovely golden toffee colour to plain meringues but for this recipe the added colours wouldn't show up.

FRESH STRAWBERRY TARTLETS

Think of those gorgeous little pastries in a French bakery – so tempting. Filled with crème patissière, they are rather more long-winded to put together, whereas the filling I've used here is just as tasty and much quicker. Strawberries are a classic topping, but raspberries or blueberries would be lovely too.

MAKES 8 TARTLETS

COOK TIME:
15 MINUTES, PLUS
CHILLING + COOLING

FOR THE PASTRY

175g (6oz) plain flour, plus extra for dusting

2 tbsp icing sugar

100g (4oz) cold butter, cubed

1 egg, beaten

FOR THE FILLING

250g (9oz) full-fat mascarpone cheese

150ml (5fl oz) pouring double cream

2 tbsp icing sugar

2 tsp vanilla extract

400g (14oz) strawberries, hulled and thinly sliced

2 heaped tbsp redcurrant jelly, for brushing

1. You will need eight 8cm (3in) round, loose-bottomed fluted tartlet tins. Preheat the oven to 200°C/180°C fan/Gas 6.

2. To make the pastry, measure the flour, icing sugar and butter into a food processor and whizz until the mixture resembles breadcrumbs. Alternatively, place the dry ingredients in a mixing bowl and rub in the butter with your fingertips. Add the egg and whizz again until you have a smooth ball of dough. Wrap the dough in cling film and chill in the fridge for 10 minutes.

3. Sprinkle a work surface with flour and roll out the dough until fairly thin – about the thickness of a £1 coin. Cut out eight discs slightly bigger than the tartlet tins. Line each tin with the pastry, on the base and up the sides (see tip), trim across the top and prick the base with a fork.

4. Line each pastry case with baking paper, fill with a few baking beans and bake blind for about 10 minutes until pale golden and starting to cook (see tip on page 210). Remove the beans and paper and return to the oven for about 5 minutes to dry out the base and to finish cooking the pastry. Set aside to cool down completely in the tartlet tins.

5. For the filling, measure the mascarpone and cream into a bowl with the icing sugar and vanilla extract and whisk by hand (see tip) until slightly thickened. Spoon some of the filling into each of the cold tartlet cases and level the top. Arrange slices of strawberry on top of each filled tartlet in a pretty spiral. Heat the redcurrant jelly in a small pan and brush over the strawberry slices to glaze.

6. Chill in the fridge for 10 minutes, then remove from the tins to serve.

PREPARE AHEAD

Can be made completely up to 4 hours ahead.
The tartlet cases can be baked up to a day ahead.

FREEZE *The tartlet cases freeze well.*

MARY'S EVERYDAY TIPS

When lining the tartlet tins with the pastry, be sure not to stretch the pastry, or it will shrink back on cooking. Handle gently and ease the excess pastry from around the edges into the sides and lip of the tin.

SCOTS WHISKY CREAM

Quick and delicious, this dish reminds me of wonderful holidays taken in Scotland over the years. Putting pared rind into the syrup while it's cooking, and then removing it once the syrup has cooled, allows the lovely orange flavour to infuse the syrup without affecting the texture of the finished cream. It's quite rich, so serve in small shot glasses or little pots.

SERVES 8–10

COOK TIME:
5 MINUTES, PLUS
COOLING

100ml (3½fl oz) whisky

100g (4oz) caster sugar

3 tbsp fine-cut orange
marmalade

Juice of ½ orange

Pared rind of 1 orange
(long strips) (see tip)

450ml (15fl oz) pouring
double cream

24–30 fresh raspberries,
to decorate

1. Measure the whisky, sugar and marmalade into a small saucepan. Add the orange juice and half the pared rind. Stir over a medium heat until the sugar has dissolved and the marmalade has melted (see tip). Bring to the boil, then allow to bubble for a minute. Remove from the heat and leave to cool in the pan for an hour.

2. Remove the orange rind from the syrup and discard. Pour the syrup into a large bowl. Add the cream and whisk, using an electric hand whisk, until soft peaks form.

3. Spoon into eight to ten clear shot glasses or cups, and top each portion with two or three raspberries and a few strips of the remaining pared orange rind. Keep chilled in the fridge until ready to serve.

PREPARE AHEAD

Can be made up to 8 hours ahead and kept in the fridge.

MARY'S EVERYDAY TIPS

The easiest way to pare the rind is with a vegetable peeler – taking off the skin but as little pith as possible. The white pith would make the flavour bitter.

When heating the syrup, make sure the sugar has completely dissolved before letting the mixture boil, or the resulting syrup will be grainy. If it starts to bubble before the marmalade and sugar have dissolved, turn the heat down and proceed on a gentle heat until ready to boil.

ROSY FRUIT COMPOTE WITH YOGHURT AND HONEY

I so love serving fruit salad as a dessert, especially when all the fruits are in season and tasting their very best. The coulis provides a lovely fresh sauce that is less sweet than a syrup, while honey-sweetened Greek yoghurt makes this a healthier treat.

SERVES 6

PREP TIME:
25 MINUTES

FOR THE COMPOTE

300g (11oz) fresh raspberries

6–8 tbsp icing sugar

150g (5oz) seedless red or
  black grapes, halved

300g (11oz) blueberries

3 nectarines, sliced (see tip)

100g (4oz) strawberries,
  hulled and quartered
  or halved

**FOR THE
YOGHURT MIX**

600g (1lb 5oz) natural
  Greek-style yoghurt

2 tbsp runny honey

1. To make a coulis for the compote, place half the raspberries in a small blender, add 6 tablespoons of the icing sugar and whizz until smooth. Push through a sieve set over a large bowl and discard the pips.

2. Add the remaining raspberries to the bowl of coulis with the grapes, blueberries, nectarine slices and stir to combine. Taste, adding a little more icing sugar if needed, depending on the sharpness of the fruit.

3. Mix the yoghurt and honey together in a separate bowl. Add the strawberries to the compote and serve with a dollop of the yoghurt mix (see tip).

PREPARE AHEAD

The compote (minus the strawberries) can be made up to 12 hours ahead and kept in the fridge. Add the strawberries just before serving.

The yoghurt mix can be made up to 2 days ahead and kept in the fridge (see tip).

MARY'S EVERYDAY TIPS

There's no need to peel the nectarines as they have tender skins. When peaches are in season, these would be just as delicious too, but peel the skins first. To loosen the skins, briefly dunk in hot water, then cold, to prevent the peaches from cooking.

For speed, you could substitute the yoghurt mix with one of the many honey-flavoured Greek yoghurts available in supermarkets.

TEATIME

Sitting down with a cup of tea and a slice
of something delicious is always so relaxing. Whether for
a quiet moment on your own, or to serve to friends, all of
the bakes in this chapter are irresistible. Walnut Brittle
and Coffee Cake (page 287) is a real crowd pleaser; or try
the Lemon and Pistachio Shortbread Biscuits (page 292)
for an everyday treat.

LEMON MERINGUE AND STRAWBERRY CUPCAKES

Think strawberry pavlova and lemon meringue pie combined in a little sponge – just too irresistible!

MAKES 12 CUPCAKES

COOK TIME:
20 MINUTES,
PLUS COOLING

FOR THE SPONGES

100g (4oz) baking spread

150g (5oz) self-raising flour

150g (5oz) caster sugar

3 tbsp milk

2 eggs

Finely grated zest of 1 lemon

7g (¼oz) freeze-dried
strawberries

FOR THE FILLING

½ jar homemade or
shop-bought luxury
lemon curd

FOR THE MERINGUE

2 egg whites

100g (4oz) caster sugar

1. You will need a 12-hole muffin tin lined with paper cases and a piping bag fitted with a plain 1cm (½in) nozzle (optional). Preheat the oven to 180°C/160°C fan/Gas 4.

2. First make the sponges. Measure the baking spread, flour, sugar, milk and eggs into a large bowl and add the lemon zest. Use an electric hand whisk to beat until light and fluffy, then fold in three-quarters of the strawberries. Spoon the mixture into the paper cases (see tip), dividing it evenly between them. Bake in the oven for 18–20 minutes or until golden, risen and springy to the touch. Set aside to cool on a wire rack.

3. When the cupcakes are cold, use a small sharp knife to cut a circle (about the width of a £2 coin) in the centre of each cake and scoop out a walnut-sized piece of sponge to leave a hole. Spoon 1 teaspoon of lemon curd into each hole, making sure the curd is level with the top of the cake.

4. To make the meringue, whisk the egg whites until stiff in a large, spotlessly clean bowl, using an electric hand whisk. Gradually add the sugar, a little at a time, continue whisking on full speed until you have a stiff glossy mixture.

5. Use a small palette knife to spread some of the meringue mixture on the top of each cupcake, or pipe the mixture on if using a piping bag, and place back in the moulds of the muffin tin. Use a blowtorch, or heat briefly under a hot grill, to lightly brown the tops of the cupcakes – watching carefully as it only takes a minute – and sprinkle over the remaining strawberries to serve. Allow to cool, and enjoy!

FREEZE *The cupcake sponges freeze well un-iced.*

MARY'S EVERYDAY TIPS

You can buy little morsels of freeze-dried strawberry in a see-through plastic tube at any good supermarket. All the moisture and liquid has been removed on freeze-drying, so the flavour is intense.

Don't over-fill the cases, as you need a little extra space to add the meringue topping once the cakes have cooled.

TOFFEE CUPCAKES

Think of sticky toffee pudding in the form of a cupcake – divine and very spoiling! Muscovado is a natural sugar and gives a wonderful caramel taste. I used light here but you could use dark muscovado, if you liked, for an even stronger toffee flavour.

MAKES 12 CUPCAKES

COOK TIME:
25 MINUTES, PLUS COOLING

FOR THE TOFFEE SAUCE

50g (2oz) butter

75g (3oz) light muscovado sugar

150ml (5fl oz) double cream

½ tsp vanilla extract

FOR THE SPONGES

100g (4oz) baking spread

150g (5oz) self-raising flour

150g (5oz) light muscovado sugar

3 tbsp milk

2 eggs

1 tbsp black treacle (see tip)

½ tsp vanilla extract

FOR THE ICING

150g (5oz) butter, softened

225g (8oz) icing sugar, sifted

1. You will need a 12-hole muffin tin and a piping bag fitted with a plain or star nozzle. Preheat the oven to 180°C/160°C fan/Gas 4 and line the tin with paper cases.

2. First make the toffee sauce. Measure all the ingredients into a saucepan and stir over a medium heat. Once the butter has melted and combined with the sugar and cream, bring to the boil and allow to bubble for about 3 minutes to thicken. Set aside to cool down completely.

3. To make the sponge for the cupcakes, measure all the ingredients into a large bowl and whisk with an electric hand whisk until blended and smooth. Spoon the mixture into the paper cases, dividing it evenly between them.

4. Bake in the oven for about 20 minutes or until well risen, golden and springy to the touch. Remove from the oven and leave to cool in the tin for a few minutes before transferring to a wire rack to cool down fully.

5. To make the icing, measure the butter and icing sugar into a bowl and whisk with an electric hand whisk until light and fluffy, or use a free-standing food mixer. Add three-quarters of the toffee sauce to the icing and whisk to combine. Keep the speed low or the sugar will fly everywhere!

6. Spoon into a piping bag and pipe swirls on top of each cupcake using either a plain or star nozzle. Use a teaspoon to drizzle the remaining sauce over the top.

PREPARE AHEAD

The cupcakes can be made 1–2 days in advance and stored in an airtight container in a cool place.

The icing can be made up to 8 hours ahead. Cover the surface to stop it drying out.

FREEZE *The sponges freeze well without the icing.*

MARY'S EVERYDAY TIP

To measure black treacle accurately, spray or coat the spoon with a little oil before scooping up the treacle from the tin. The treacle will then slip off easily when you add it to the bowl.

CHOCOLATE REFLECTION CAKE

This impressive-looking cake is perfect for any celebration. The sponge is easy to make, so put all your efforts into the beautiful icing. Chocolate icing can loose its sheen if kept in the fridge for too long, but adding the gelatine is what gives this cake its wonderfully shiny surface, enabling it to keep its gloss.

SERVES 10

COOK TIME:
25–30 MINUTES,
PLUS COOLING

FOR THE SPONGE

50g (2oz) cocoa powder

90ml (3fl oz) boiling water

3 eggs

175g (6oz) self-raising flour

1 tsp baking powder

100g (4oz) baking spread,
  plus extra for greasing

250g (9oz) caster sugar

FOR THE ICING

7 sheets (11g) of leaf
  gelatine (see tip)

225g (8oz) caster sugar

75g (3oz) cocoa powder

75ml (2½fl oz) double cream

50g (2oz) dark chocolate,
  broken into pieces

2 tbsp apricot jam,
  for brushing

**TO FILL AND
DECORATE**

300ml (10fl oz) double
  cream, softly whipped

10 strawberries with their
  green tops

1. You will need two 20cm (8in) round, loose-bottomed cake tins with deep sides. Preheat the oven to 180°C/160°C fan/Gas 4, then grease the tins with baking spread and line the bases with baking paper.

2. Sift the cocoa powder into a large bowl. Pour in the boiling water and stir into a smooth paste. Add the remaining ingredients and beat together using an electric hand whisk until light and fluffy. Spoon into the prepared tins and level the tops.

3. Bake the cakes in the oven for 20–25 minutes (ideally on the same shelf, so that they cook at the same rate) until well risen and coming away from the sides of the tins. Transfer to a wire rack to cool for 10 minutes, then remove the baking paper and leave to cool down completely.

4. To make the icing, soak the gelatine leaves in a bowl of cold water for 5 minutes until soft. Measure the sugar, cocoa powder and cream into a saucepan and pour in 125ml (4fl oz) of water. Stir the mixture over a gentle heat until the sugar has dissolved, then bring to the boil and continue to stir until smooth.

5. Remove from the heat and add the chocolate pieces to the hot liquid, allowing them to melt. Leave to cool for 5 minutes. Remove the gelatine leaves from the bowl of water and squeeze out any liquid before adding to the pan. Stir the warm chocolate mixture until the gelatine has dissolved, then pour through a sieve into a bowl. Place in the fridge to cool down for about an hour and thicken to the consistency of thick mayonnaise.

6. Slice each sponge in half horizontally. Spread a third of the whipped cream over one layer of sponge, followed by another layer of cream and sponge, and continue to assemble the cake until you have four layers of sponge and three of cream. Press the sponges down between each layer so the cream comes right to the edges and the sponges are level at the sides. Take a palette knife and smooth around the edges so the excess cream very lightly covers the sides and gives a smooth edge.

Recipe continues overleaf

7. Warm the apricot jam in a small saucepan and then pour through a sieve to remove any lumps. Brush the warmed jam over the top the cake (see tip), then chill in the fridge for 15 minutes.

8. Pour 50ml (2fl oz) of the icing into a bowl, then dip the top half of each strawberry into the melted icing and set aside on baking paper to set.

9. Pour or spoon the remaining icing over the top of the cake, smoothing it over the top and sides with a palette knife. Be very careful doing this – you want a smooth shiny icing (see tip). Leave for an hour or so to set.

10. Arrange the chocolate-iced strawberries around the bottom edge of the cake to serve.

PREPARE AHEAD

The cake can be fully made and iced up to a day ahead and kept in the fridge.

FREEZE *The sponges freeze well.*

MARY'S EVERYDAY TIPS

Leaf gelatine comes in various sizes now so it is best to check it by weight.

The apricot jam 'seals' the cake and any loose crumbs, so that the icing has a smooth surface to cover.

When icing the cake, use long slow strokes with your palette knife to give the best finish. If a stray crumb gets on the palette knife, wipe it off with kitchen paper before retouching the cake. And if the chilled chocolate icing has thickened too much on sitting, give it a good beat with a spoon at room temperature to loosen it up again.

WALNUT BRITTLE AND COFFEE CAKE

Classic coffee and walnut cake is always such a favourite. Here I've given it an extra twist by using walnuts made into a delicious caramel praline. Using the all-in-one method for the sponge means this cake is very straightforward to make and much quicker with the help of a food mixer, but be careful not to over-mix or the sponges may not rise properly. Just beat until combined for a wonderfully light cake.

SERVES 8–10

COOK TIME:
40 MINUTES, PLUS
COOLING

FOR THE SPONGE

225g (8oz) butter, softened (see tip), plus extra for greasing

225g (8oz) caster sugar

225g (8oz) self-raising flour

1 tsp baking powder

4 eggs

1 tbsp instant coffee mixed with 2 tbsp water

FOR THE WALNUT BRITTLE

50g (2oz) walnut pieces

75g (3oz) white caster sugar (see tip)

FOR THE BUTTERCREAM

150g (5oz) butter, softened

450g (1lb) icing sugar, sifted

2 tbsp milk

2 tsp instant coffee mixed with 1 tbsp water

1. You will need two 20cm (8in) round, loose-bottomed sandwich tins. Preheat the oven to 180°C/160°C fan/Gas 4, then grease the tins with butter and line each of the bases with a disc of baking paper.

2. To make the cake, measure all the ingredients into a mixing bowl and mix with an electric whisk, or use a free-standing food mixer, until smooth and just combined. Divide the batter between the prepared tins and level the surface of each with the back of your spoon.

3. Bake in the oven for about 25 minutes or until golden and well risen. Set aside to cool down completely before turning out of the tins and peeling off the baking paper.

4. Meanwhile, make the walnut brittle. Add the walnut pieces to a dry pan and toast over a medium heat for 3–4 minutes, tossing frequently to ensure they don't burn, until golden. Tip into a bowl.

5. Add the sugar and 2 tablespoons of water to a stainless steel saucepan. Stir over a low heat until the sugar has dissolved and the liquid is clear. Discard the spoon, increase the heat and boil for about 5 minutes until golden and caramel-coloured. Remove from heat (it will continue to deepen in colour), then quickly tip in the toasted walnuts. Shake the pan, then pour on to baking paper to cool.

6. Once the brittle is cold, put half into a food processor and whizz into a fine powder. Use the end of a rolling pin to bash the remaining brittle into chunky pieces.

7. To make the buttercream, measure the butter, icing sugar and milk into a bowl and add the coffee. Beat using an electric hand whisk until light and fluffy, then add the powdered brittle and stir to mix in.

Recipe continues overleaf

8. To assemble the cake, spread half the buttercream on one sponge, top with the other sponge and spread with the remaining buttercream. Scatter the rest of the walnut brittle in a ring around the top to decorate.

PREPARE AHEAD

Can be fully assembled up to 6 hours ahead. Once sandwiched together with the buttercream, the cake will last for 2–3 days in an airtight container, but the brittle may start to soften, so best to decorate on the day of serving.

The buttercream can be made up to 2 days ahead; cover the surface to keep it soft.

FREEZE *The sponges freeze well without the buttercream.*

MARY'S EVERYDAY TIPS

Soft butter is essential for an all-in-one cake. If using butter straight from the fridge, you can soften it in a microwave on the lowest possible setting, taking care that it doesn't melt. A safer method is to cut the butter into cubes and leave in a bowl of lukewarm water for 5–10 minutes.

As it's a refined sugar, with no impurities, white caster sugar is preferable for making caramel.

Use a stainless steel pan to make the caramel.

MIXED SEEDED SNAPS

These thin, crispy golden treats are great for a picnic or packed lunch. The key to making them is to dissolve the sugar slowly, then boil without stirring. It's also important to caramelise the sugar sufficiently so that it 'snaps' rather than bends. Once it's reached this stage, you'll then need to work quickly to spread it out before it sets. So you need to take a little care over this one, but the end results are well worth it!

MAKES 24 SNAPS

COOK TIME:
10 MINUTES, PLUS COOLING

Butter, for greasing

150g (5oz) caster sugar

150ml (5fl oz) golden syrup

250g (9oz) mixed seeds (such as sesame, sunflower and pumpkin), toasted (optional)

1. You will need a 25 x 30cm (10 x 12in) Swiss roll tin or baking tray. Line the tin with non-stick baking paper.

2. Measure the sugar and syrup into a wide pan and heat gently and slowly until the sugar has dissolved and the mixture is clear.

3. Bring the mixture to the boil and boil for 2–3 minutes, without stirring, until it begins to caramelise and turn golden in colour (see tip).

4. Remove the pan from the heat to prevent the mixture from caramelising further, then add the seeds, and stir until coated. Quickly tip the mixture into the buttered tin and flatten/spread with a palette knife right up to the edges of the tin until the mixture is perfectly level, thin and even (see tip).

5. Use a sharp knife to lightly score 12 squares (3 x 4). (Try not to cut right through the mixture – you don't want to mark the tin.) Score each square in half diagonally to give 24 triangles. Leave to cool completely, remove from the tin then cut/snap along the score lines and enjoy.

PREPARE AHEAD

Can be made up to 3 days ahead and kept in an airtight container.

MARY'S EVERYDAY TIPS

Boiling the sugar and syrup for a couple of minutes will take it to a temperature of 130–150°C (265–300°F), the 'hard crack' stage of caramelisation. Test with a sugar thermometer, if you have one, or drop a little of the molten mixture into a bowl of cold water. It should form hard, brittle threads that snap when you bend them.

You will have to work quickly to spread the mixture and cover the whole surface of the tin, as it needs to be thin to give the best results. It's quite tricky to spread, but persevere; it gets easier as it starts to cool slightly, though it needs to remain warm and pliable. You've got a window of 5–10 minutes before it sets. Once it's spread, then you can score it.

LEMON AND PISTACHIO SHORTBREAD BISCUITS

Shortbread must be my favourite biscuit of all time – I just love the crunch and crumbly texture. Perfect to have in the cupboard for an everyday treat when someone pops in. Anyone who has been to our house will tell you a plate of shortbread always appears!

MAKES 20 BISCUITS

COOK TIME:
15 MINUTES, PLUS COOLING

175g (6oz) butter, softened

75g (3oz) caster sugar

175g (6oz) plain flour, plus extra for dusting

75g (3oz) semolina

Finely grated zest of 1 lemon

25g (1oz) shelled pistachio nuts, finely chopped

1. Preheat the oven to 200°C/180°C fan/Gas 6 and line two baking sheets with baking paper.

2. Measure the butter, sugar, flour and semolina into a food processor, add the lemon zest and whizz until combined. Tip the dough on to a floured work surface and knead until smooth.

3. Split the dough in half and roll each piece into a long sausage shape – about 15cm (6in) long. Scatter the chopped pistachios on a plate and roll each dough sausage in the nuts to coat. Cover the rolls and chill for 30 minutes.

4. Slice each roll into ten even-sized discs. Arrange on the prepared baking sheets, well spaced apart as they will spread slightly during cooking.

5. Bake in the oven for about 15 minutes, until just tinged golden and almost firm to the touch. Carefully transfer to a wire rack to cool and firm up.

PREPARE AHEAD

Can be made up to 3 days ahead and kept in an airtight container (see tip).

FREEZE *The cooked biscuits freeze well.*

MARY'S EVERYDAY TIP

When storing homemade biscuits, place kitchen roll in between each layer of biscuits. This prevents them from going soggy. If they have become soft, or have been defrosted after freezing, place on a baking sheet and refresh in a low oven to bring them back to life.

ORANGE OAT COOKIES

Great for that everyday cup of coffee! Adding the egg gives the cookies a softer, more cake-like texture, rather than crisp like shortbread. The icing makes them a bit more special too, and they have a lovely fresh orange flavour.

MAKES 12 COOKIES

COOK TIME:
12–15 MINUTES,
PLUS COOLING

100g (4oz) butter, softened

200g (7oz) self-raising flour, plus extra for dusting

25g (1oz) rolled oats

100g (4oz) caster sugar

1 egg

Finely grated zest of 2 oranges

100g (4oz) icing sugar

1–2 tbsp orange juice

1. Preheat the oven to 180°C/160°C fan/Gas 4 and line two baking sheets with baking paper.

2. Measure the butter into a large bowl with the flour, oats and sugar and add the egg. Add three-quarters of the orange zest and mix to combine. On a work surface lightly dusted with flour, roll into 12 equal-sized balls.

3. Sit the balls on the prepared baking sheets, spaced well apart from each other (they will spread during cooking), and flatten slightly with the palm of your hand to about 1cm (½in) thick.

4. Bake in the oven for 12–15 minutes or until lightly golden and firm (they will crisp up once cooled). Leave to cool for 5 minutes on the baking sheets, then use a fish slice to transfer them to a wire rack to cool down completely.

5. Sift the icing sugar into a bowl, then gradually mix in enough of the orange juice to make a smooth icing with a drizzling consistency.

6. Drizzle the icing in zigzags over the cold cookies (see tip) and while the icing is still wet, scatter with the remaining orange zest.

PREPARE AHEAD

Can be made up to a day ahead and kept in an airtight container.

FREEZE

The cookies freeze well. Once defrosted, crisp up in a low oven to serve.

MARY'S EVERYDAY TIP

Leave the cookies on the wire rack while you drizzle over the icing, and put a baking sheet underneath to catch any drips.

WEEKEND FRUITCAKE

The lemon and spice give this lightly fruited cake a lovely fresh flavour. It is a real classic that will last for a good couple of weeks if you store it in an airtight container in a cool place – if the family can keep their hands off it for that long! Leave in the tin to cut – the first slice will be just as good as the last.

SERVES 8

COOK TIME:
11/2–2 HOURS,
PLUS COOLING

100g (4oz) glacé cherries

225g (8oz) butter, softened,
   plus extra for greasing

225g (8oz) light
   muscovado sugar

4 eggs

225g (8oz) self-raising flour

50g (2oz) hazelnuts, toasted
   (see tip) and finely chopped

Finely grated zest of
   2 lemons

1 tsp mixed spice powder

1 tsp ground cinnamon

100g (4oz) currants

100g (4oz) sultanas

25g (1oz) flaked almonds,
   to decorate

1. You will need a 20cm (8in) round, loose-bottomed cake tin, at least 5cm (2in) deep. Preheat the oven to 160°C/140°C fan/Gas 3, then grease and line the base and sides of the cake tin.

2. Quarter the glacé cherries, wash and dry thoroughly on kitchen paper. Place all the ingredients except the cherries, dried fruit and flaked almonds in a large bowl and mix well with a wooden spoon. Add the cherries, currants and sultanas and fold in to combine (see tip). Spoon into the prepared tin and scatter over the flaked almonds.

3. Bake in the oven for 1½–2 hours (see tip) until well risen and set on top, evenly browned and when a skewer inserted into the middle of the cake comes out clean. Cover with foil after 1 hour, if getting too brown.

4. Leave to cool in the tin for 10 minutes, then remove the sides of the tin and turn out the cake. Remove the base of the tin and the baking paper and leave the cake to cool on a wire rack.

PREPARE AHEAD

Can be made up to 2 weeks ahead. Store in an airtight container.

FREEZE *Freezes well.*

MARY'S EVERYDAY TIPS

To toast hazelnuts, spread on a baking sheet and pop in the preheated oven for 5–10 minutes while preparing the other ingredients and the tin. Keep an eye on the nuts during cooking to ensure they don't burn – toss on the baking sheet if necessary. Allow to cool slightly and chop before adding to the bowl. Alternatively, use ready-roasted chopped hazelnuts.

Washing and drying the cherries, and folding all the dried fruit into the batter after the other ingredients, helps to prevent the fruit from sinking to the bottom of the cake during cooking.

Check the cake after 1½ hours, as it can dry out if left for the full 2 hours.

GINGER AND MANGO SPICED MUFFINS

These look and feel pretty healthy – very different from sweet muffins covered in frosting. They're perfect for breakfast on the go, or for a lunch or teatime treat. The addition of ginger and mango makes a wonderful flavour combination. Delicious on its own as a snack, dried mango comes in packets like sultanas from supermarkets or health-food shops.

MAKES 12 MUFFINS

PREP TIME: 20 MINUTES

COOK TIME:
25 MINUTES, PLUS
COOLING

150g (5oz) light
muscovado sugar

225g (8oz) self-raising flour

50g (2oz) rolled oats, plus
extra for sprinkling

2 tsp mixed spice powder

1 tsp baking powder

100g (4oz) dried mango, very
finely chopped

2 balls of stem ginger, rinsed
and very finely chopped
(see tip)

1 egg

100ml (3½fl oz) vegetable oil

175ml (6fl oz) milk

1. You will need a 12-hole muffin tin. Preheat the oven to 200°C/180°C fan/ Gas 6 and line the tin with paper cases.

2. Place the sugar, flour, oats, spice and baking powder into a large bowl add in the mango and ginger, then stir to combine. Break the egg into a separate bowl and beat with a fork. Add the oil and milk to the eggs and mix to combine.

3. Add the wet mixture to the dry mixture and beat with a wooden spoon to combine. Try not to over-beat or the muffins will be tough. Divide the mixture evenly between the paper cases and sprinkle a few extra oats on top.

4. Bake in the preheated oven for about 25 minutes or until golden, well risen and springy to the touch. Allow the muffins to cool for a few minutes in the tin before transferring to a wire rack to finish cooling.

PREPARE AHEAD

Can be made up to a day ahead.

FREEZE *The muffins freeze well.*

MARY'S EVERYDAY TIP
Jars of stem ginger in sugar syrup are easily available, though you could use crystallised ginger instead.

HUMMINGBIRD CAKE

The addition of fresh-tasting pineapple in this Southern US classic takes banana cake up a notch. It makes for a moist, substantial cake, beautifully offset by the tangy cream cheese icing.

SERVES 8–10

COOK TIME:
25–30 MINUTES, PLUS
COOLING + CHILLING

FOR THE SPONGE

250g (9oz) self-raising flour

250g (9oz) caster sugar

1 tsp baking powder

1 tsp ground cinnamon

50g (2oz) walnut
  pieces, chopped

2 large ripe bananas, peeled
  (200–250g/7–9oz peeled
  weight) and mashed

1 x 432g tin of pineapple
  chunks, drained and finely
  chopped (see tip)

2 eggs, beaten

1 tsp vanilla extract

175ml (6fl oz) sunflower oil,
  plus extra for greasing

FOR THE ICING

100g (4oz) butter, softened

175g (6oz) full-fat cream
  cheese (see tip)

300g (11oz) icing
  sugar, sifted

1 tsp vanilla extract

1. You will need two 20cm (8in) round, loose-bottomed sandwich tins. Preheat the oven to 200°C/180°C fan/Gas 6, then grease the tins with a little sunflower oil and line each of the bases with a disc of baking paper.

2. Measure the flour, sugar, baking powder and cinnamon into a large bowl, add the chopped walnut pieces and stir together. In a separate bowl, mix together the mashed bananas and chopped pineapple with the eggs, vanilla extract and sunflower oil. Add the banana/pineapple mixture to the dry ingredients and stir with a wooden spoon to combine, taking care not to over-mix.

3. Divide the batter evenly between the prepared tins, smoothing the tops with your spoon, and bake in the oven for about 25–30 minutes or until golden, well risen and springy to the touch. Set aside to cool down completely before turning out of the tins and peeling off the baking paper.

4. To make the icing, place the butter in a bowl with the cream cheese, icing sugar and vanilla extract and beat together with an electric hand whisk until smooth. It is best to beat in the icing sugar a little at a time so that it doesn't fly everywhere. Chill the icing for 30 minutes before assembling the cake.

5. To assemble the cake, place one cold sponge on a plate or cake stand and spread with half the icing, then sit the other sponge on top and spread with the remaining icing.

PREPARE AHEAD

This cake will keep for a day or two at a cool room temperature.

FREEZE *The sponges freeze well.*

MARY'S EVERYDAY TIPS

To save time, use a mini food processor to chop the pineapples.

Take the cream cheese out of the fridge to soften before making the icing, or beat to soften first.

ORANGE DRIZZLE CAKE

A simple, but perfect treat for everyday, this is a cross between a drizzle cake and a Victoria sandwich – a winning combination! The crunchy drizzle topping always goes down well.

SERVES 8

COOK TIME:
25 MINUTES, PLUS
COOLING

FOR THE SPONGE

4 eggs

225g (8oz) caster sugar

225g (8oz) self-raising flour

225g (8oz) baking spread,
plus extra for greasing

1 tsp baking powder

Finely grated zest of 1 orange

**FOR THE
DRIZZLE ICING**

Juice of ½ orange

100g (4oz) caster sugar

Grated zest of ½ orange
(grated using a zester),
to decorate

**FOR THE
BUTTERCREAM
FILLING**

100g (4oz) unsalted
butter, softened

Finely grated zest
of ½ orange

2 tbsp orange juice

150g (5oz) icing
sugar, sifted

1. You will need two 20cm (8in) round, loose-bottomed sandwich tins. Preheat the oven to 180°C/160°C fan/Gas 4, then grease the tins with baking spread and line each of the bases with a disc of baking paper.

2. To make the icing, mix the orange juice and sugar together in a bowl.

3. To make the sponges, place all the ingredients for the batter in a bowl and whisk together with an electric hand whisk until combined. Divide the mixture evenly between the prepared tins and level the tops.

4. Bake in the oven for about 25 minutes until golden brown and springy to the touch. After 5 minutes turn out of the tins, remove the baking paper and transfer to a wire rack. Immediately pour the drizzle icing on top of one sponge (see tip), all the way to the edge. Sprinkle with the orange zest (see tip) and set aside to cool down completely.

5. To make the filling, place the butter in a bowl with the orange zest and juice. Adding the icing sugar a little at a time, whisk with an electric hand whisk until smooth.

6. Sit the plain, non-iced sponge on a plate and spread over the buttercream, right to the edges. Place the drizzle-iced sponge on top to sandwich the cakes together. Cut into wedges to serve.

PREPARE AHEAD

Cake can be assembled up to 8 hours ahead.

FREEZE

The sponges freeze well – remember to wrap in cling film then tin foil.

MARY'S EVERYDAY TIPS

It is important to pour the drizzle icing on top of the warm cake so the juices run into the sponge, keeping it moist. Stand the cake over a baking sheet to catch the drips or pour the syrup over the sponge while it is still in the tin, so none is lost.

It's also important to sprinkle the orange zest over the top of the sponge immediately after the drizzle icing, or the zest will dry out as the cake stands. Alternatively, decorate with zest just before serving.

SULTANA SCONES

This recipe makes eight beautifully risen, large scones, though you could use a smaller cutter to make more scones. The correct way of serving a scone is to break it in half with your hands, rather than cutting it with a knife, and serve with the cream and jam on the side.

MAKES 8 SCONES

COOK TIME:
12–15 MINUTES

2 eggs

About 225ml (8fl oz) milk

450g (1lb) self-raising flour, plus extra for dusting

2 rounded tsp baking powder

75g (3oz) butter, softened (see tip)

50g (2oz) caster sugar

25g (1oz) sultanas

TO SERVE

Strawberry jam

Clotted cream

1. You will need a 8cm (3in) fluted pastry cutter. Preheat the oven to 220°C/200°C fan/Gas 7 and line two baking sheets with baking paper.

2. Break the eggs into a measuring jug, beat together with a fork and then pour in enough milk to give you 300ml (10fl oz) liquid.

3. Measure the flour, baking powder and butter into a large bowl. Rub the butter into the flour with your fingertips until it looks like breadcrumbs. Tip in the sugar and enough of the liquid (you may not need it all) to make a sticky dough. Add the sultanas and mix with your hands until combined.

4. Tip on to a floured work surface and gently knead until it comes together. Use a rolling pin to roll out the dough to about 2.5cm (1in) thick. Using the pastry cutter, stamp out eight discs (see tip), re-kneading and rolling the trimmings as necessary, and arrange on the baking sheets, spaced a little apart. Brush the tops with any leftover liquid from the jug.

5. Bake in the oven for 12–15 minutes or until well risen, golden on top and slightly browned underneath. These are best served warm, fresh from the oven, with the strawberry jam and clotted cream.

PREPARE AHEAD

Best made on the day, but can be made a day ahead and then warmed in a low oven to serve.

FREEZE *The scones freeze well.*

MARY'S EVERYDAY TIPS

If using cold butter from the fridge, fold back the wrapper and grate the butter straight into the mix, then stir it in.

Dip your cutter in flour if it starts getting sticky. When stamping out pastry discs, do not twist the cutter or the scones will rise unevenly. A general rule is fluted cutters for sweet, plain for savoury.

CONVERSION TABLES

MEASUREMENTS

METRIC	IMPERIAL
5 mm	1/4 in
1 cm	1/2 in
2.5 cm	1 in
5 cm	2 in
7.5 cm	3 in
10 cm	4 in
12.5 cm	5 in
15 cm	6 in
18 cm	7 in
20 cm	8 in
23 cm	9 in
25 cm	10 in
30 cm	12 in

OVEN TEMPERATURES

°C	FAN °C	°F	GAS MARK
140°C	Fan 120°C	275°F	Gas 1
150°C	Fan 130°C	300°F	Gas 2
160°C	Fan 140°C	325°F	Gas 3
180°C	Fan 160°C	350°F	Gas 4
190°C	Fan 170°C	375°F	Gas 5
200°C	Fan 180°C	400°F	Gas 6
220°C	Fan 200°C	425°F	Gas 7
230°C	Fan 210°C	450°F	Gas 8
240°C	Fan 220°C	475°F	Gas 9

Both metric and imperial measures are provided – always follow one or the other, never mix the two.
Spoon measures throughout the book are level unless otherwise stated. Use a set of measuring spoons for accurate measuring.
All eggs used in recipes are large unless otherwise stated.

VOLUMES

METRIC	IMPERIAL
25 ml	1 fl oz
50 ml	2 fl oz
85 ml	3 fl oz
100 ml	3½ fl oz
150 ml	5 fl oz (¼ pint)
200 ml	7 fl oz
300 ml	10 fl oz (½ pint)
450 ml	15 fl oz (¾ pint)
600 ml	1 pint
700 ml	1¼ pints
900 ml	1½ pints
1 litre	1¾ pints
1.2 litres	2 pints
1.25 litres	2¼ pints
1.5 litres	2½ pints
1.6 litres	2¾ pints
1.75 litres	3 pints
1.8 litres	3¼ pints
2 litres	3½ pints
2.1 litres	3¾ pints
2.25 litres	4 pints
2.75 litres	5 pints
3.4 litres	6 pints
3.9 litres	7 pints
5 litres	8 pints

WEIGHTS

METRIC	IMPERIAL
15g	½ oz
25g	1 oz
40g	1½ oz
50g	2 oz
75 g	3 oz
100 g	4 oz
150 g	5 oz
175 g	6 oz
200 g	7 oz
225 g	8 oz
250 g	9 oz
275 g	10 oz
350 g	12 oz
375 g	13 oz
400 g	14 oz
425 g	15 oz
450 g	1 lb
550 g	1¼ lb
675 g	1½ lb
750 g	1¾ lb
900 g	2 lb

INDEX

A

ale
  beef and ale stew 87–8
anchovies
  salsa verde 107
apples
  apple and lemon galette 240–2
  blackberry and apple crumble pie
    235–6
  pear and apple crumble 233
  potato salad with celery and apple 209
  steamed golden apple pudding 232
artichoke hearts
  artichoke and garlic dip 52
  avocado, artichoke and feta salad 213
  rice salad 151
  artichokes, Jerusalem *see* Jerusalem
    artichokes
Asian dressing 93
asparagus
  smoked haddock and asparagus
    chowder 67
aubergines
  aubergines and Taleggio bake 183
  melanzane pasta 180–2
avocados
  avocado, artichoke and feta salad 213
  chicken satay salad 222
  guacamole with coriander 50
  individual smoked salmon and prawn
    starters with avocado 75

B

bacon
  chicken Valencia 137
  crispy bacon rösti with fried egg 80
  griddled chicken carbonara 130
  tartiflette 205
  see also pancetta
baking blind 242
bananas
  hummingbird cake 300
  passion fruit and banana Eton mess
    265
barley *see* pearl barley
basil
  salsa verde 107
batch cooking 11
bay leaves 24

bean sprouts
  chicken satay salad 222
  chicken stir-fry 126
  five spice salmon stir-fry 154
beans
  chilli con carne 89
  squash and black bean chilli 179
béchamel sauce 180–2
beef
  beef and ale stew 87–8
  chilli con carne 89
  curried beef samosas 44
  fillet beef salad with Asian dressing 93
  fillet steak with peppercorn sauce 90
  ragù bolognese with pappardelle 94
beer
  beef and ale stew 87–8
beetroot
  beetroot chutney 76
  beetroot houmous 53
  three beetroot salad with mozzarella
    and basil 218
biscuits 25
  lemon and pistachio shortbread
    biscuits 292
  mixed seed snaps 291
  orange oat cookies 295
black beans
  squash and black bean chilli 179
blackberry and apple crumble pie 235–6
blinis
  herbed blinis with peas and
    pancetta 71
blueberries
  rosy fruit compote 273
Bolognese sauce 94
bread 25
  dill, herring and quail's egg canapés 33
  goat's cheese bruschetta 214
  mushroom bruschetta 68
  poppy seed croutons 64
breadcrumbs 159
  panko breadcrumbs 146
  very posh fishcakes 145–6
broad beans
  green beans and mangetout 202
  orzo with broad beans, peas, lemon
    and thyme 185

broccoli
  broccoli and cauliflower stir-fry 206
  warm bulgar wheat and quinoa
    broccoli salad 221
bruschetta
  goat's cheese bruschetta 214
  mushroom bruschetta 68
bulgar wheat
  herbed quinoa and wheat salad 217
  warm bulgar wheat and quinoa
    broccoli salad 221
butter 25
  garlic herb butter 49
  mint caper butter 202
  softening 288
buttercream
  coffee 287–8
  orange 303
butternut squash *see* squash

C

cabbage
  green vegetable stir-fry 198
cakes 25
  chocolate reflection cake 283–4
  hummingbird cake 300
  lemon meringue and strawberry
    cupcakes 279
  orange drizzle cake 303
  toffee cupcakes 280
  walnut brittle and coffee cake 287–8
  weekend fruitcake 296
canapés
  curried beef samosas 44
  dill, herring and quail's egg canapés 33
  dough balls with garlic herb butter 49
  ginger and chilli tiger prawns 53
  smoked salmon, red pepper and
    spinach bites 37
  spiced chicken and chicory boats 42
  spicy Mexican samosas 45
  Thai crab poppadom canapés 34
capers
  mint caper butter 202
caramel
  mixed seed snaps 291
  toffee cupcakes 280
  toffee sauce 245

THE BIGGEST OF THANK YOUS

Lucy Young, where do I begin to thank someone who has been by my side for 27 years. Lucy has the patience of a saint, keeping me on my toes, deciphering all my recipe ideas and notes and is meticulous in everything she does. I cannot get away with anything! I cannot thank her enough.

Lucinda McCord for testing our recipes, such a talent we could never be without, you are loved by us all.

Georgia Glynn Smith has produced the magical photography in many of my books – she is exceedingly talented and makes it all fun at the photo shoots.

Jo Penford, the skill behind my make up, which I moan about as it takes too long, but she is the best there is. Jo is never idle, makes the best coffee and always gives a helping hand. A treasure to be with.

Lisa Harrison and Isla Murray, book shoot and TV home economists – top of their tree and second to none, thank you – a perfect duo.

Charlotte Macdonald – what a delight to work with, and the caring lot at BBC Books, meticulous and dedicated.

Karen Ross, Emma Boswell, Dave Crerar and the team at Sidney Street Productions who made the series to accompany the book. There is no better, kinder, more patient a team, thank you for making it a joy.

Back at home, Kathryn Demery, doing our business side and holding the fort in the office amongst endless pieces of paperwork.

My family and close friends who are always behind me, taking part in picnics and parties for the TV and book. I know the family think it is a great bonus to be the tasting panel and enjoy the leftovers!

Thank you,
Mary B
xxx